QUESTIONS YOU MAY BE ASKED!

First impression *1946*
Reprinted *1948*
Reprinted *1957*
Reprinted *1980*

Printed in Great Britain by
Lowe & Brydone Printers Ltd, Thetford, Norfolk

QUESTIONS
YOU MAY BE ASKED!

WINIFRED MOYES

Published by
THE GREATER WORLD ASSOCIATION TRUST
3 Lansdowne Road, Holland Park, London W11 3AL, England

ZODIAC

A Teacher at the Temple in the Time of Our Lord

Spirit picture of Zodiac when in an earth body, as
seen through the mediumship of Miss Ida Dixon.

The name of Zodiac was chosen by this guide simply to lift our thoughts
from the earth to the stars. His earth name has not been disclosed, but
he has revealed that he was the scribe mentioned in St. Mark xii, 28-34.

Winifred Moyes

FOREWORD

People in many parts of the world have read the addresses by Zodiac ever since "The Greater World" was founded in 1928, and in Great Britain nearly 600 friends received them in type-written form for years before the paper was started. Many have expressed the hope that a summary of the teaching embodied in the addresses might be published, and two or three students kindly attempted the task. They found, however, that Zodiac at different times had dealt with so many aspects of each subject that, in spite of their utmost care, important points relating to the Truth might be overlooked by them and, therefore, the responsibility of undertaking the work was too great.

A Church of England Rector in a country parish, who had spare time, asked if he might have all the addresses given by Zodiac over the years for the purpose of analysing them. We gladly consented. After studying them for nearly a year he wrote saying that again and again he thought he had discovered contradictions of thought, but on referring to his notes he found that the point in question was still another angle of the subject and had its rightful place. He expressed the opinion that it was impossible for any physical mind to produce the addresses and also to maintain such a standard of consistency in the teaching over the years.

Zodiac's method of imparting spiritual facts has been based, as far as possible, on the perfect method adopted by The Master, Who gave revelation to the world in language that every one could understand, using the common incidents of daily life as similies of Divine Truth. Language can be a dangerous tool, and simple facts are presented sometimes with such an elaboration of words that very few can understand what is meant; whereas words were intended to be employed by the expert so that technical facts or intricate subjects could be explained in simple terms. Such word-builders are the inspirers of mankind, but they are few and far between. Christ was indeed a master of this precious art!

In July, 1945, I was urged by Spirit-helpers to make time to respond to the earnest desire of so many readers to have a summary of Zodiac's teachings. It was perhaps easier for me to undertake this task than for anyone else because over the years I have had to proof-read two or three times each one of his addresses before publication, and so know "by heart" the many aspects of Truth revealed by him. Moreover, in our private Circle, Zodiac has given us an outline of Divine Law which relates to Life in every world. We were told that by applying the principle of this Law to any question asked, we should be able to give a logical and practical reply; and we have found that this is so.

"Questions You may be Asked" is presented with the sympathetic desire to help not only Church Leaders and Mediums, but also men and women generally who find it hard to reconcile their difficult lives with a God of Love. The "Answers" are based on Divine Truth, which transcends all creed and doctrine; therefore they should be acceptable to people of every religious belief. During the War we were asked innumerable questions by members of the three Forces. One and all said they found no difficulty in agreeing with our commonsense replies. Many had trained minds, and their instinct for Religion had suffered severely because so often what they had heard associated with religious teaching clashed with their reasoning powers and sense of justice.

Knowing that it was useless to overload the mind of the enquirer with a mass of spiritual facts, I have endeavoured to give, so far as possible, " nutshell explanations " only of the various subjects of interest arising out of Spirit return and communion; and, for the purpose of easy reference, to deal with them in alphabetical order.

The explanations are offered as a possible help in thinking things out and not with any intention of " laying down the law." We recognise that each individual is entitled to his or her own point of view, and the last thing we wish is that these " Answers " should be used to cause dissension. There are many roads to God — this is essential because of varying temperaments and inheritances of race and creed. But there is this inescapable fact — that whatever path is chosen, the only way to progress spiritually is by service and sacrifice. So Divine Law overrules all the inequalities of human life in regard to intellect, limitations of health and opportunity.

INDEX

Questions

you may be asked!

ABSOLUTION (the power to remit sin).—Through repentance a sinner becomes reunited in love to God; but sin leaves consequences, for what a man sows he will reap. The Cross of Jesus Christ represented not a blood-sacrifice but a Love-sacrifice, and it must be remembered that although the physical body is capable of great suffering, its sensitiveness cannot be compared to the greater sensitiveness of the real self. (*See* CALVARY.)

ACCIDENTS.—Many are caused by heedlessness or recklessness. Therefore in order to co-operate with our Spirit helpers who seek to protect us, we should try to exercise care and aforethought. But all disasters bring a spiritual compensation. Unavoidable accidents are classed among the trials of human life, and comfort comes from the realisation that only by personal experience of suffering can our sympathies be enlarged and the power be won to help others.

AFFINITIES.—At creation in the far past each child of God had a "counterpart," but lives may be lived separately in many worlds before affinities are reunited. This great gift has no relation to physical attraction between the sexes on the earth plane. The link of affinity is a spiritual one, in which the physical senses have no place. The long separation between the "counterparts" is entirely for the purpose of the development of character. If life on earth represented a condition of love and harmony very little would be learned. Understanding is acquired only by meeting and overcoming what is in opposition to ourselves. The reality of our love, faith and hope can be tested only by that which assaults those high gifts. (*See* GENESIS ch. 1, ver. 27.)

AGNOSTICISM.—*See* ATHEISM.

AMBITION.—Is it wrong to have material ambitions? No; we are meant to exercise our mental and physical gifts, and through the discipline thus imposed, many spiritual attributes can be released—patience, endurance and the will to work. The mistake made is in limiting ambition to earthly things. Man's capacity was meant to be far greater, and his power to create of a much higher order than that shown upon the earth plane; and this will be possible as he evolves in other worlds. Gradually, as we progress, the meaning of real ambition, and the gifts housed in our divinity, become revealed to us.

ANGELS.—Celestial beings are not separate creations; they represent God's children who have striven much harder for spiritual release than we have. They need not necessarily have had an earthly body. Angelhood is dependent always upon the high degree of love and service forthcoming. By living a spiritual life NOW, after the transition we need not remain in any astral world, but can pass through those gates into spiritual conditions. This law is exampled in regard to angelic beings. By the tremendous effort they made for emancipation, the lessons of the lower spheres had already been learned, and they passed into the pure realms of Spirit.

ANIMALS.—All animals, which are a separate creation, have their place in the Divine Plan. The earth-world is but one stage of experience, and the creatures on this plane have states of deterioration and evolution even as man. When created, each form of life was perfect, because out of Perfection—God—imperfection could not emanate. Survival is a fundamental of Divine Law; and animals, birds and beasts, after undergoing experiences on earth, will also manifest in a finer form in the next stage, the degree being dependent largely upon their discipline and sufferings while on earth. With domestic animals, the degree of love and obedience shown to their owners ensures enhanced forms of life after physical death.

APPARITIONS.—The difference between an apparition and a Spirit-being is that the first may be a thought-form only, while the second definitely is a soul free from the physical body. Ghosts are associated with terror simply because those who saw them knew nothing about "survival." Many of them were earth-bound souls drawn back into their old conditions by the remembrance of some crime or serious mistake. The knowledge of the continuity of life and the many prayers sent out by thousands of Spiritualists for earth-bound souls may account for the fact that apparitions or ghosts are seldom seen to-day.

ASTRAL.—This word describes conditions created by the senses, not necessarily "evil" conditions, but they can become very dangerous when the individual is governed by his baser self. In the aura surrounding this world there are many astral conditions, but a mighty cleansing power is provided also through all the sorrow and pain endured by so many on earth. There are other spheres which are far more astral than the earth, but there are innumerable Spirit spheres free from this contamination. Spirit teachers urge us to cleanse our gifts and desires while in the flesh, so that our powers hereafter are unfettered and we have the joy of harmonising with pure conditions.

(The meaning of "astral" has somewhat changed over the years, but it was always employed to express the next body or world after the physical state. The emanations from the material self—desires for this and that arising from the human side—congregate by the law of attraction around the earth. The vibrations are not necessarily "bad," but eventually desire and emotion will be lifted above the personal and gradually brought into harmony with the spiritual self.)

ASTROLOGY.—Man is not a blind instrument of Fate. The planetary system exerts its influence on physical life because, for the purpose of the development of character, souls are born at certain times of the year as well as in a particular environment. The Spirit within man has had life in different bodies in uncountable worlds before the earth came into use for the furtherance of God's Plan, and we choose our own experiences in each stage, free-will being a gift from the Creator. Knowledge of planetary "influences" also enables us to be on our guard against weak or dangerous characteristics, and misfortunes brought about by man's own fault often can be avoided by watchfulness over certain tendencies in our nature. In fact, the Divine within man is lord even of the horoscope !

ATHEISM AND AGNOSTICISM.—The atheist says : "There is no God" ; the agnostic—"I do not know if there is a God." Beliefs or opinions are, however, of far less importance than ACTIONS. To have no consciousness of God is a great loss to man while in the body, but if he does his best for others that "blindness" of mind will not persist after physical death ; the transition will reveal to him a God of infinite Love. But atheists or agnostics who destroy the faith of others find that rectification entails great suffering and effort.

AURAS.—Man is body, soul and spirit. Within man is Divinity ; around the fleshly body there is a protective covering called the aura, varying in size, colour and strength according to the spiritual evolution of the one concerned. The aura has many functions, including a transmitting and receiving "station," allowing man not only to receive healing rays or impressions, but to send them out to others. The aura represents the map of the life that is lived ; in fact, it is the replica of the soul-body which we shall inhabit after physical death, and on its health will depend our future happiness. Every form of life has its own aura and this relates to all worlds.

BADNESS.—Why are some people bad and others good? It depends on the release of the Divine within us, and, again, this depends on the effort made by the individual to progress. Undeveloped souls, or "bad" people, bring a lot of trouble upon others, but much more upon themselves eventually. The victims of environment or of training are responsible only for what was their own fault. Man not only has a second chance after physical death, but many chances to retrieve. The postponing of rectification means, however, that during that period he is forfeiting spiritual health and happiness in whatever world he finds himself.

BAPTISM.—Some people say that it is taking advantage of helplessness to baptise children in their infancy; that this should be left to free-will later on. But baptism combines gratitude to God for the child and an active desire for spiritual protection over the young life. Parents and god-parents take on the responsibility of leading the child into the right path; in this way good habits are formed which may have a tremendous influence when maturity is reached. During the early stages the life within each tiny body is at the mercy of the older ones, and the result of their guardianship has to be faced later on.

BEAUTY.—An exquisite sunset taxes to the uttermost the emotional side of us which responds to beauty. As our consciousness expands we shall be able to contact with higher and still higher forms of beauty. Those who have seen anything of the Summerland, which is the first state beyond the earth plane, find earthly words of description entirely inadequate so amazingly lovely are the flowers, forests, lakes and seas. These are among the many wonderful things God has provided for His children who, in time, will become "all glorious within."

BEGGARY.—This is a reality in other worlds as well as on earth, the difference being that here abject poverty is caused by lack of material means; after physical death it is the lack of spirituality. Another distinction is that on earth material means can be given or stolen; on the Other Side it is impossible to take what is not ours and, moreover, although progressed spirits may be willing to share their good gifts, the capacity to TAKE depends entirely on our response to spiritual things.

BENEDICTION.—The word "blessing" is very freely used; but those with clear vision can see how holy power, represented by glorious Spirit hues, descends upon an individual or upon a congregation. For the full grace of a benediction to be expressed there must be a linking up with the Spirit World between the one who bestows and the one who receives. The greatest blessings have been manifested when least expected, very often being given to prepare those in the body to meet great trials of strength and endurance.

THE BIBLE.—These records represent mediumship in its highest form, for the facts were written down long after the events happened. Recent excavations have proved that what were regarded as legends must have been true. That psychic gifts were recognised in those days is borne out by the records of clairvoyance, clairaudience and the many prophecies which, later on, were fulfilled. Here and there in the Bible there are incidents which seem a denial of Divine Love. These are signs of an inaccurate memory or of a faulty mediumship. But the more the Bible is studied the greater grows our admiration over those wonderful mediums of the long ago who, so arduously, wrote down what they were told, little dreaming that their labour would bring spiritual understanding to the many generations to come. Spirit teachers assure us that if the words of Our Lord could have been written down as He spoke them, there could have been no division in thought among the Christian sections. How grateful we should be to the scribes of old who have enabled us to share the comfort and illumination of the Master's life on earth and His most loving teaching.

BIRTH.—All creation has innumerable births and deaths. Man died to a previous state in another world to be born into the earth plane, and he must die to a physical world to be born into a spiritual state, and so on through uncountable stages. Great preparations are made by the angelic ministry in regard to birth and death, and the greatest care is taken to safeguard the entry of a soul from one state into the next.

BROTHERHOOD.—The law of brotherhood is an ideal, and we know that in some future state the earthly obstacles to "brotherhood," expressed by religion, race and language, will gradually pass away. In the meantime we can try to broaden our sympathies with those of other opinions and outlook on life, keeping ever in mind the fact that we are all children of the one Father, and that the time will come when the barriers made by different stages of progression will be bridged by true love. Outstanding examples of the brotherhood spirit are shown again and again in times of famine, pestilence and disasters.

CALVARY.—Explanation was given under "Absolution" regarding the nature of the sacrifice which the crucifixion of Our Lord expressed. The word "crucified" is used in a general way to denote a heavy cross of trouble. Among the experiences of every evolving soul there must be included, although in a much lesser degree, those endured by the Master Christ, because He came to show us "the way." Only by entering our garden of Gethsemane, where we strive to gain the strength to accept our cross and to go through with all it represents, can the resurrection of the real self be assured and spiritual freedom made our own. So temporary loss is turned into eternal gain.

CELESTIAL.—A Divine or Heavenly state. St. Paul speaks of celestial and terrestrial bodies, "terrestrial" expressing different grades of density. Many mediums have the gift of celestial vision and they are able to describe what can be termed the "outer" courts of Spirit Realms. Their type of clairvoyance allows them to see those who have passed over in something of their ethereal state;

for these mediums it is not necessary for the spirits to "clothe" themselves in the garments of the earth in order to ensure recognition. This gift was the possession of some of the early disciples, and has been manifested throughout the ages in many saints and martyrs, who have been baffled in the task of finding the right words to express what has been opened to their vision because the earth holds no parallel as regards colour, fragrance or melody.

CEREMONY.—Simple ceremony is part of everyday life, such as courtesy shown to a guest or to those who are ill or old. Ceremony is bound up in the traditional life of all countries; but putting aside the strong influence of custom, we come to the purpose of its use, which is to express "respect." Spirit teachers emphasise that in the degree that it enables a soul to feel in closer contact with God so ceremony is justified; but there are many who find that it raises barriers, that the actions involved by ceremony distract the mind from its object, which is the linking up of the child with the Father. Therefore its usefulness depends upon the temperament. There are many roads to God and everything that helps man in his spiritual evolution is blessed.

CHILDLESSNESS.—One of the great sorrows of earthly life is the lack of a child in the home, and it has been noticed that those who would make ideal parents are the ones very often who are bereft of this gift. But the earth-world is only one of countless worlds in which we have lived; and if the lessons of parenthood have already been learned in a previous state, souls anxious to increase their experience may, in Spirit, have willingly diverted their energies to another task. But their homes are full of Spirit children who claim them as their parents ! In reality, there are no childless people, no orphans and no lonely ones, for "parenthood" and all it involves, is the Law of Life. Suffering is caused because, owing to the material conditions of this plane, Spirit sight and hearing are limited. God's most loving plans for progression rest on the aid given by "parents" (*more mature souls*) to weaker types of the same life and to other forms of life; and wise parents on earth illustrate, in degree, the law of parenthood which is in operation throughout all states and worlds according to their evolution. Many on earth instinctively "mother" or "father" those who are not their own by ties of relationship; this is universal in Spirit Life.

CIRCLE.—Because a circle has no beginning or end it is employed as a symbol of protection as well as an indication of a spiritual life. Over the generations great artists of religious pictures have used a circle of light around the head of an apostle or a saint to indicate that the life has been devoted to service. To a developed medium the circle, or halo—often shown in beautiful rainbow colours—is an index to the character of the one concerned. For the development of spiritual gifts the habit of sitting in a circle is general. Sometimes the members hold hands, but this is unnecessary for protection as the link between the sitters is not a physical, but a spiritual one. The only way that full protection can be maintained is by being "one-minded" over the elimination of self.

CLAIRAUDIENCE AND CLAIRVOYANCE.—Spirit hearing and sight have brought comfort and illumination to many thousands of people; but the release of these gifts on constructive lines entails discipline and suffering, both essential to develop the character so that, mentally and emotionally, the instrument is strengthened and not weakened in the process of becoming accustomed to sights and sounds of other worlds. Spirit sight and hearing cannot be restricted to what the medium wishes to see and hear. Life is made up of good and evil in varying stages; and some who could have become good instruments have allowed fear to cut short their development. But the burying of these talents must bring "consequences" in the hereafter. A wise guide warns his instrument that certain tests of courage and faith will have to be met, and at intervals these trials take place, the medium gradually working through reluctance and gaining the ability to apply spiritual law, which eventually enables her not only to be willing to minister to unevolved spirits, but to gain a real influence over them. On the other hand, Spirit hearing and sight, when used not for self but for others, bring the medium into touch with indescribably beautiful conditions of love and power; and those who have heard the "heavenly choirs" will never forget the unutterable happiness of that experience.

COLOUR.—Spirit vision, as it develops, reveals marvels in regard to colour, which in more evolved worlds supersedes speech, colour being a visible expression of thoughts and feelings. Speech is a clumsy tool and the cause of much misunderstanding, for it can be used to hide the truth; but in Spirit Realms thoughts and feelings manifest in colours around the individual and, therefore, deception is impossible. But although the higher colour-vibrations cannot be seen with the physical eye, they can be sensed; hence a depressed or sulky person is described as being in a "brown" study—a dark and dense colour. The colours seen upon the earth plane are expressed in much lovelier hues in other worlds, light or "glory" in varying degrees being their essence or background. Spirit vision reveals a host of colour-rays which have no parallel with those seen in Nature, and we are told that in the higher realms there are exquisite colour-vibrations far beyond our physical consciousness to grasp. Clairvoyants may differ over the colour of the garment of a highly evolved guide, but they may all be accurate, for as different subjects are dealt with by the "control," each one brings its own particular colour-ray, and, therefore, the "garment" or the aura quickly changes in hue.

CONCENTRATION.—Prayer and concentrated thought represent the foundation of spiritual healing and also are essential for the safe development of psychic gifts. Wonderful visions are witnessed during these "quiet times."

But concentration should not be allowed to take the place of "doing." Good thoughts are constructive, but good actions are better still. The ideal is to see that Spirit inspiration is transmitted into definite acts of service.

CONFESSION.—Some people find great relief in telling another about their misdeeds; it means "a burden shared is a burden halved." And when those who listen are true servants of the Christ, much help and strength can be passed on, and the culprit feels in a measure cleansed of his sin. But it is not within the power of anyone in the body, or free from the body, to sweep away the consequences of misdoing. Where great assistance can be given is in showing how the one concerned can, by service to others, "work out" what has been done. In this way spiritual progress, and all the joy it brings, need not be unnecessarily delayed. As with ceremony, so with confession; if it helps any soul to make a closer contact with God, then it has its use.

CONSEQUENCES.—The law of cause and effect is a reality in every world. Sometimes on earth Divine Justice is questioned because there are no immediate consequences of good or ill, but consequences must be met either here or hereafter, for the record of our lives is registered in Spirit conditions. One act of good or evil in this world is one act only, bringing either gain or loss. Even if a crime has been committed it has no detracting influence on the good deeds that stand to a man's credit. God does not punish us; it is we ourselves who inflict the punishment, for by the abuse of free-will we cannot vibrate to peace and joy, and, therefore, are drawn into those conditions where there is only a limited degree of happiness and freedom. Consequences, or "retribution," is the law of mercy, for only through suffering can we break free from the bondage of self.

CONTINUITY.—Spirit teachers emphasise the continuity of Life through all the different worlds. We "die" to one state to be "born" into the next. A temporary

cessation of activity can occur through lack of knowledge. After physical death the individual may seem to be
in a coma for some time, for determined disbelief in an
After-Life brings consequences. But the Divinity within
never ceases to struggle for freedom, and by the ministrations of Spirit helpers the coma-state can be shortened so
that the one concerned can commence upon the great
work of reconstructing thoughts and ideas about God
and the gift of Immortal Life.

DIRECT CONTROL BY THE CHRIST.—Several people
have asked if this is possible. We gladly give the facts
according to Divine Law :

It is obvious that everything that is GOOD has its
primary source in God. Between us and the Creator
there is a chain of Life from very highly evolved spirits,
right down the scale of progression to those on the earth
plane, all acting as intermediaries. Through this living
chain flows Divine Power—healing and spiritual knowledge—until it reaches those who are gifted with mediumship in a physical body when, again, the power is passed
through them to many others, and so on. It must be
remembered that everything that is "good" has life everlasting and that earthly mediums represent only one
more link in that great Chain of Life. All Spirit messages
which have an inspiring effect on others can be claimed
to come in the first place from God, or from that ap-
proachable manifestation of God which we have in
Christ. But to be used as a medium through whom a
Divine ray can be passed is very different from the claim
that Christ takes control of a physical body and speaks
directly through it. In the first place, this would be in
opposition to the law of vibration. As souls evolve, so
their rate of vibration is enhanced; in comparison with
the activity in the Spirit Worlds, life on the earth-plane
seems as a slow-motion picture. This illustrates the
barriers and limitations of the physical body; and also
the difference between the high altitude of celestial
beings and the lower altitude of those undergoing their

earthly experiences. The holy ones who come back to us have to "re-clothe" themselves with dense matter in order to key their vibrations, or emanations, to our clouded auras; and without this harmonising there can be no direct control. Human beings, with their limited degree of spirituality, can contact with only a portion of the purity of highly evolved souls; but if there is an earnest desire within them to do good, that tiny link acts like "a hook and eye" between the instruments in the body and the bright ones sent back to minister to those on earth. It must not be forgotten that mediums act as valuable links between the spheres of Light and the earth plane, and also with worlds that are less evolved than the physical.

God has ordained that the only way of spiritual progression is by service to others. Therefore the great chain of Life from God to man, in its varying stages of evolution, means that everyone in that chain is fulfilling the Law, in degree. We know that God, or Christ—into Whose hands the Father delivered "all-power" (ST. MATTHEW ch. 28, ver. 18)—could do anything without the aid of intermediaries; but the Creator, out of His great Love instituted that Law which limits His own Power, namely—that He works only through the life He has brought into being, AND NOT INDEPENDENTLY OF IT. Thus, Divine Law rules out direct control by the Christ. Apart from the fact that the physical body could not survive contact with so much Holiness, direct control by Our Lord would nullify Divine Law; indeed it would be working in opposition to it. But by the employment of intermediaries through whom "good" can be radiated, the law of progression—which is service to others—is in full operation.

CAN THE HOLY ONES OF OLD CONTROL MEDIUMS TO-DAY?—This question has been asked by a reader, and the answer may be of general interest. The only barriers between the earth and the Spirit World are those erected by mankind. The separation, life from life, in the different worlds, is not according to the Divine Plan. Each world or condition converges on the other, and the Spirit within us can go where it will according to the measure of its release from bondage. God never intended that there should be suffering caused by the transition of souls from one state to another; the change of body and condition was meant to represent the reward for seeking to overcome trouble and striving for spiritual emancipation.

Christ said : "Blessed are the meek for they shall inherit the earth." To many this promise conveys nothing, for they see the humble-hearted often bearing the heaviest burdens and bereft of possessions. But The Master's words reveal a great spiritual fact. Those who are patient under their sufferings and place their confidence in God and not in themselves, do "inherit" the earth after their transition. They can return, in spirit, to the physical world and go where they will, and have the inexpressible joy of acting as missionaries. Their gifts are many and their "inheritance" is richer in value than the human mind can grasp. This explains why it is possible for the holy ones of old and the saints and martyrs to come back into these material conditions; and also it is one of the strongest arguments against the belief that souls re-incarnate into other physical bodies and have many lives on earth.

But the fact that the holy ones can return does not mean that every spirit controlling a medium and claiming to be a disciple of old is genuine. The early Christians were accustomed to the exercise of psychic gifts and St. John gave an explicit warning to the Churches of that time on this important point, saying : "BELIEVE NOT EVERY SPIRIT, BUT TRY THE SPIRITS WHETHER THEY BE OF GOD ; BECAUSE MANY FALSE PROPHETS ARE GONE OUT INTO THE WORLD."

"By what method can controlling spirits be tested?" many may ask. The answer is simple and given by The Master Himself : "BEWARE OF FALSE PROPHETS WHICH COME TO YOU IN SHEEP'S CLOTHING, BUT INWARDLY THEY ARE RAVENING WOLVES. YE SHALL KNOW THEM BY THEIR FRUITS !"

The same method of "testing" the character of spirits holds good for those inhabiting a physical body. There are those we know, or have heard of, in daily life who call themselves Christians, and yet on occasions are vindictive and treacherous in their actions.

Undeveloped spirits do sometimes take control of inexperienced or unspiritual mediums; but by prayer and the gift of discernment they can be detected in due course. Enthusiastic and inexperienced sitters, who have not studied either Divine Law or psychic law, have been deceived in this way; but according to the measure of their sincerity and devotion, protection has been given; and the lesson once learned is invaluable as others can be warned and so safeguarded. As there are "impersonators" on earth so there are impersonators in worlds which are less evolved than the earth, and instruments prone to vanity may become easy prey. It is impossible for a medium who is used by a highly evolved spirit to feel personal satisfaction; to a certain extent there must be some affinity of ideals between the controlling spirit and the one who is controlled. Therefore if a medium claims that he or she is used by a holy one of old and yet lacks humility, the statement can be rejected. There are "guides" who assert that they are important teachers, and that their instruments are wonderful mediums. These spirits condemn themselves. Remembering how much we have been taught by those in Spirit Life concerning spiritual Truth, as well as having the written record of The Master's life and words, we are all poor mediums in comparison with the heights risen to by the first disciples and the early Christians, who did not hesitate to choose martyrdom rather than deny their faith. It would be impossible for a holy one of old to give messages showing either boastfulness or dictatorship. Spiritual evolution is expressed by love, humility and understanding, and this is the "test" which provides evidence to the sitters regarding the character of a controlling spirit.

But another point must be remembered: that all that is good must come in the first place from the Source of Goodness—GOD—and the "message" has been passed on through innumerable intermediaries, from the holy ones down the evolutionary scale until it reaches the earth, each messenger sharing in the blessing. This is essential because with our present limitations of Spirit consciousness we can assimilate only a fragment of the goodness which the higher spheres of Light represent. (*See* REINCARNATION.)

CREMATION.—Does cremation represent a shock to those whose desires are still centred on earthly things? Spirit teachers tell us that the destruction of the physical casket can be an aid to earth-bound souls as its annihilation brings home the impermanency of the material body and the foolishness of attaching so much importance to it ; also it destroys a fettering link between the individual and his earthly conditions, and this may induce him to explore the conditions in which he finds himself. Those who have led an ordinary good life quickly become at home in the Spirit World, for over the years they have often been there during the sleep state. The fate of the fleshly body seems of no importance at all ; in fact, in comparison with their new body it represents something from which they are glad to be free.

DAMNATION.—The old belief that sinners are condemned to everlasting punishment reflects the cruelty in human nature in presenting such a God of vengeance. Teachers from the World of Spirit emphasise that not only does man have a "second chance" after physical death, but there are no limits to the opportunities provided to bring about his spiritual release. Yet the law of consequences is inescapable. This, however, is mercy, because God cannot learn our lessons for us. Only by the suffering which sooner or later follows wrong-doing, can man find that the way into Peace is by observing Divine Law. The origin of man was God; his ultimate destiny is to be reunited to God in love. By the abuse of free-will —which is possible in all worlds—his self-inflicted punishment is to be in those dreadful conditions which are a "materialisation" of his own thoughts and actions. But ministering angels hover around seeking to release in the bonded soul some response to better things.

DEATH.—Death is the law of life because only by dying to one condition or state can the changes associated with growth take place. The grief and horror linked to the death of a loved one is caused not only by a sense of loss over the physical presence, but still more because of the mystery which enshrouds the After-Life. Parents sent their children across the seas for the war-years; they knew where they were and received messages from them; and, at times, through the radio, heard their voices. The children were missed, but the parents were at peace because the young folk were protected. It should be the same with those who pass into the Spirit World. Their welfare is assured; they can send messages through trained instruments and their voices can be heard by clairaudients. Moreover, those in a physical body, when asleep, can be with loved ones in the Spirit World for part of each 24 hours. This law applies also when both are on this side, but separated by distance. The earth and physical body represent but one experience only out of innumerable experiences in different worlds and bodies. We died to a previous conscious existence to be born into a material body; we die to the earth-world to be born into brighter conditions, where we shall have a more ethereal body if we have done our best. The abuse of free-will does not alter the fact of death; but it has its repercussions on the next state, for as a man sows he must reap. The law of life and death has been in operation since our creation in the far, far past, and will continue until we have reached Perfection, when no more deaths will be necessary as we shall have attained Life in its immortal sense.

DEMONS.—Clear vision reveals spirits who are so unprogressed that they might be termed demons; but although fallen from their high estate they are still the children of God and heirs to everlasting life. Their conditions are appalling for "like attracts like," and they find themselves surrounded by those as cruel and vindictive as they are themselves. There are no defenceless victims in the dark spheres ! This means that each one tries to inflict greater punishment on the other than he himself has to endure; and fear is the mainspring of these attacks. However, this extreme suffering is the best friend of the one concerned because it eventually brings something of purification to the aura. There are spirit "doctors" waiting to rescue those who desire to be rescued, and from then onwards, so far as co-operation can be enlisted from the patient, a gradual improvement can take place. The appearance of souls in the demon-state is terrifying to the clairvoyant if compassion is not stronger than personal fear. Only very experienced mediums can be employed as intermediaries by the guides for missionary work among those in such bondage, but they ARE found and are used both in the trance state and during the hours of physical sleep for this most vital rescue work.

DEVELOPMENT.—A word employed in regard to the unfoldment of the faculties represented by trance mediumship, clairaudience and clairvoyance, which implies that a higher intelligence from the Spirit World can "tune into" the vibrations of an instrument in a physical body. The degree of at-one-ment is revealed by the accuracy of the mediumship. Just as some have a talent for music or painting, so others have the right kind of sensitiveness to become a good medium. But training is essential to bring about an understanding of the rules which govern the expression of any gift; and as tuition regarding the fine arts requires a very experienced teacher, so it is essential that any guide who is allowed to exercise an influence over the souls of others should be very highly evolved in a spiritual sense. In the New Testament it is written : "Believe not every spirit, but try the spirits to see whether they are of God." "Controls" who show anger, changeability or ambition can be deemed unfit for teachership, and more spiritual guides should be sought. They are always available, but, again, "like attracts like." Some people are natural mediums, which means that second sight and hearing are part of their make-up. These instruments require special safe-guarding as their gifts, having entailed no discipline or suffering in their release, may not be regarded as a sacred trust. Slow and sure unfoldment is best, so that maturity may reveal that development of character has kept pace with the release of mediumship. (*See* MEDIUMSHIP.)

DISCIPLINE.—This is essential for a progressive life in this world or in any other; and if mankind as a whole could see in discipline the short road to success, the evolution of the earth plane would be hastened. Good crafts-manship necessitates a strict training, and that imposes a severe discipline on the one concerned; but once the craft has been mastered, joy comes in creating. The tool of the human mind represents but a shadow in com-parison with the higher intelligence of emancipated souls. Emancipation is brought about by understanding Divine Law, and understanding can be won only by enduring the discipline of learning

DISEASE.—The theory of heredity—the inheritance of disease from ancestors—is a modern version of the message given through that amazing medium, Moses, and embodied in the Ten Commandments: that the iniquity of the fathers would be visited upon the children to the third and fourth generation of those who hate God, but mercy would be shown to thousands who seek to keep His commandments. If the law of brotherhood had been observed over the generations, disease, poverty and crime would be unknown. Physical suffering on a gigantic scale prevails because the germs of disease have been passed on by ancestors through lack of self-control over drinking, eating and other weaknesses of the flesh. Those who ignore Divine Law to-day are also jeopardis-ing the health and happiness of children perhaps of the third and fourth generation to come. So the innocent suffer through the guilty! But we have the glorious promise that mercy will be shown to thousands who keep God's commandments. This Law has been exampled by the results of spiritual healing; and miracles of Grace have been shown by sufferers of every race, for the Divine within has been manifested by the faith and courage shown by them. If the roots of disease have gone too deep for a cure, then comfort comes from the thought that all suffering contributes great strength and beauty to the soul-body which will be donned as physical death takes place.

DISFIGUREMENTS.—Physical deformity, wound scars, birthmarks and skin troubles which can be seen by others, are often the cause of a depression amounting to despair. They have changed the course of physical life for the sufferers and are closely associated with fear, for so often love is forfeited through them. The saying that "beauty is only skin deep" seems to mock the afflicted; and every effort should be made to pass on the comfort which Spirit teaching alone can give, so that the next body may not be marred by too many bitter thoughts souring the temperament.   Deformities and disfigurements on the soul-body are a reality; in fact, far more repulsive diseases are shown on it than those brought about by the ills of the flesh. But these are the fault of the one concerned, for they represent deliberate wrong-doing during the earth life. Whereas those in the physical body who have endured this martyrdom—often through the sins of their forbears—find after the transition that their soul-body is amazingly healthy and beautiful.

DIVINING.—People who know nothing about mediumship sometimes possess this form of psychic power. It allows them to sense or foretell where water-springs, oil-wells, and even precious minerals, lie deep beneath the earth, and the gift is of great value especially when the finding of water has become a necessity. The divining rod—the shape of a wishbone—was first made of hazel and then of witch-elm. An end of the fork is held in each hand, and when the right spot of ground is

reached it is claimed that the rod-portion bends towards
the earth. Some who understand psychic power feel that
the divining could be done by a "sensitive" without the
aid of the divining-rod, but it serves a useful purpose by
acting as a point of concentration.

DREAMS.—Dreams result from many causes —
physical ailments, mental worries and sudden shocks to
the emotions. But dreams can also represent a faint
remembrance of where the freed Spirit has been when the
body has been asleep. When the burdens of the day are
heavy, or the health is poor, it would not always be wise
to put an extra strain on the physical consciousness which
the remembrance of such dreams involve; but wonderful experiences of Spirit-travelling have been recorded,
showing the degree of at-one-ment possible between the
material and spiritual selves. Freak dreams are often the
result of physical disturbances, but they can occur
through the fact that the Spirit on returning to the body,
has to pass through the astral "belt" or aura which surrounds the earth; and if the physical mind is not trained
to discriminate, the dreams appear to be a mixture
of stupidity and wisdom, which is not surprising when
remembering the medley of thoughts and emotions cast
into the earth's aura by the millions of men and women
over the ages.

EARTH-WORLD.—As this is the only world we know
with the physical mind, it is difficult to keep a sense of
proportion over its relative importance or unimportance.
But it must be remembered that the earth is but one
state out of countless worlds. As St. Paul said : "There
are celestial bodies and bodies terrestrial . . . for one star
differeth from another in glory." The texture of the
physical body and its organs are essential to allow us to
breathe and grow in these material conditions; therefore
it is commonsense to accept the fact that in all the other
worlds we have bodies suitable to the conditions there.
The earth is certainly an important "class" in the great
School of Life because it is possible not only to exercise

free-will, but through the measure of Spirit-consciousness which it is within our scope to release here, the
experiences of this state can further our progress in a
very valuable way. The promise of life in celestial bodies
in celestial worlds holds out a future of higher and still
higher ranges of peace and happiness. (*See* EVOLUTION.)

ECTOPLASM.—This word is used in connection with
psychic phenomena to express an emanation—like clouds
of varying density — which comes from the medium.
This ectoplasm can be materialised in so definite a
manner that it can be seen, touched and photographed.
Often a spirit-form appears out of an ectoplasmic
envelope, implying that this mould of psychic power had
to be drawn together to allow the form to become visible
to material sight. Physical mediumship demands a great
deal of vitality from both medium and circle, but these
materialisations have been used to bring conviction of
survival. The same psychic power raised to a higher level
could be employed for spiritual healing, and, bearing in
mind the terrible suffering in the world to-day, those
who are told they could develop physical mediumship
are reminded that it is also within their capacity to become powerful healers. (*See* MATERIALISATIONS.)

EDUCATION.—Life in the different spheres represents
stages of education in its spiritual sense if the individual
accepts the opportunities provided. The training of the
mind during the earth-state can contribute much towards
that higher form of education which concerns character,
and the discipline of temperament exacted by the acquire-
ment of knowledge when on earth will be most useful
in other worlds. But there are many kinds of discipline
which those in a physical body encounter, and the ones
denied a mental education will find themselves at no disadvantage after the transition if their souls have become
"educated" by trouble and suffering. Spiritual development does not depend upon the number of talents or gifts
possessed, but upon the use made of even one talent or
gift; and it is logical to say that there is far more credit

due to the man poor in equipment but rich in courage, than to the one provided with many kinds of help through being born into an environment where there was plenty of everything.

EGO—the "I" that thinks, feels and acts; but the point is HOW the individual thinks, feels and acts; and this depends upon the safeguarding or the abuse of free-will. The "ego" can express the Divine within man, when the individual becomes a great power in the world for good. On the other hand, by the concentration on self to the exclusion of the community, the ego so domin-ates all other attributes that the mind becomes diseased and, finally, unbalanced. Hitler and Mussolini are recent examples of how men of ability can lose everything through inordinate vanity.

ELEMENTALS, or "elementary" spirits.—This term is used in regard to souls to describe those who are in such an elementary stage of evolution that they are far below anything seen on earth. The reason for this con-dition is because in the many other worlds in which they were intended to acquire useful experience, no effort was made to progress. But Divinity is within them in the same measure as it is in the saints—it is a case of its im-prisonment by selfishness, or the release of holiness by sacrifice. Elementary spirits are seen by many mediums used for rescue work; some appear in such distorted forms that they seem to be half beast and half reptile. There are others who cannot be described as there are no earthly parallels. Can these souls ever be redeemed from their fallen state? They MUST be released from their bondage as there are no spirits who are "lost" indefinitely. Their influence depends entirely upon the free-will of the ones they seek to captivate. But the only way in which to influence them is through that deep compassion which is an expression of love. Mediums at first are over-come by fear when they see clairvoyantly these dreadful beings; but gradually, by practice, fear—which springs from the instinct of SELF-preservation—gives way to the

missionary spirit, which desires above all things to save !
Much can be done by prayer, but the prayer should not
be for personal protection from the bound spirit, but for
the release of the tormented one. Only very experienced
mediums should undertake this missionary work. Many
of these souls are not sufficiently evolved to have under-
gone the earth experience.

EQUALITY.—To understand equality in its rightful
sense one has to break free from the remembrance of the
many inequalities associated with earthly life—race, sex,
and worldly possessions being the most obvious. Education has allowed certain races to forge ahead of those who
are ignorant; but the training of the human mind, if its
powers are wrongly used, means that after physical
death even a genius may have become an imbecile. In
contrast those who have been educated by sorrow and
pain and hardship—which released sympathy and understanding during the earth life—find in the next stage that
they possess a high intelligence and can be entrusted with
important work. It must be remembered that in all worlds
the Law of compensation and retribution is a reality, and
although hidden from human sight the readjustments are
made immediately in regard to "loser" and "gainer."
Over the generations sex has provided a great barrier to
equality; but in the New Testament it is shown that Our
Lord, ignoring a rigid custom of that time, addressed
some of His most revealing remarks to women. In Spirit
Spheres the goal of every progressing soul is to develop,
individually, the highest qualities associated with the
man and the woman which, together, represent a completed soul, when the one concerned enters into angelhood.

ETHEREAL.—Conditions and qualities associated
with a more highly evolved state than the earth. But, as
with all things, there are stages of etherealism or spirituality. The glorious scenes of Spirit Life revealed by clear
vision are merely as the "outer courts" of Paradise, for
the things God has prepared for His children transcend
our present sight, hearing and understanding. We are

told that certain Spirit guides are co-operating in preparing their earthly instruments so that they may see disembodied spirits in as much of their ethereal state as
human limitations allow.   It is wise for those on earth to
forget the diseased and worn-out bodies of those so dear,
and to visualise them as young, strong and beautiful.
Evidence of identity would be supplied by portraying the
personality of the communicating spirit. In this way
impersonations would become impossible. The facts concerning our lives on earth are known by many on the
Other Side, and the submitting of such details does not
necessarily represent "watertight" evidence; but it is
impossible to imitate the individuality of another. We
understand that when the earth conditions become sufficiently clarified "etherealisations" will take the place of
"materialisations." This means that it may be possible
to raise the rate of vibrations in a Circle to that degree of
purity that those who have passed over can appear in
their ethereal "bodies." Many mediums have clairvoyant
visions of those on the Other Side in this rarified state;
but the material conditions of the earth prevent the
physical eyes from seeing these wonderful manifestations, although they are all around us.

EVOLUTION—includes the progress of all forms of
life on earth and in all the spheres until perfection is
attained. Many people accept the theory that man has
evolved not only from the ape but that he has progressed
through a multitude of stages from the merest speck of
life on the sea shore. But Spirit teachers remind us that
the earth is but one sphere alone out of innumerable
worlds. They emphasise that the Story of Creation
(GENESIS, ch. 1, 2 and 3) should be read as a parable out-
lining the truth; that we were created in the Divine Image
long before the earth plane came into use for the evolution of God's children. We were gifted with free-will,
but the one important thing lacking was experience, and
in the degree that it was absent so also was understanding missing. The reason for man's fall from the Divine
Image is indicated in the parable of the Garden of Eden,

where the temptation came to eat of the fruit of the forbidden tree in order to become "gods." The symbolism
used refers to lust for power, and over the ages, and also
to-day, man has succumbed to this temptation. Uncountable lives in other worlds have been the lot of us all—
the earth representing but ONE short stage—and our
present state of evolution shows how far we have protected or abused the gift of free-will. Although there may
be similarities, the different forms of life—animals,
creatures and Nature—represent separate creations
undergoing their evolutionary stages. What we see now
is but one aspect of that particular form of life. Perfection will ultimately be attained by all creations. Man was
given dominion over every other form of life, but this
power was forfeited in the measure that he lost dominion
over his lesser self. In the degree that he regains self-
mastery, so will he obtain that wise authority over all
other life which represents true guardianship.

FAIRIES.—Through Spirit teachers we glean a few
facts regarding fairies and all those included among the
"Little People." Apparently there are many kinds of life
unknown to our physical minds, but every species has its
helpers as well as its enemies, and suffering is used, as
with man, to further progression. Fairies, elfs, gnomes,
etc., are not "thought-forms," or imaginary beings; they
have their own place in the great scheme of Life. Many
are highly intelligent and are capable of feeling joy or
sorrow; but some still seem to be acting from instinct
only. They vary also in appearance, but, in miniature,
they resemble the human form. Some of the fairies are
under one inch, but the gnomes are a foot high or more.
A great many people with clairvoyant vision have
watched these delightful little folk, and these confirm that
their tiny forms are in perfect proportion, they are often
quaint but never gross. The "garments" of the fairies are
of exquisitely delicate shades, but the elves and gnomes
are seen in vivid autumn colours. The Little People
represent the helpers of Nature, but as they progress they
take a great interest in human beings and what they are

doing. But it is beyond our scope to understand the vast work carried through by the many millions of fairy-folk. Acting either from instinct alone, or, later, from instinct to which is added intent, they are certainly "doers," and they suffer when, through lack of our co-operation, they cannot do their part. Undoubtedly there are those in authority and those who obey, but they all work under a "law," even as the bees and ants. If there are naughty fairies and gnomes, they seem to be kept in the background so far as humans are concerned, and so all our memories of this form of life are sweet. We love them for themselves and we are very grateful to them for the many ways in which they try to help us. Definite mediumship is shown by the writers of fairy tales, who have been used to make known that the little folk exist; also wonderful prophecies have been given through these stories, which are as parables containing great truths.

FATE.—Many people have been brought to a state of depression and even of despair because they believe they are at the mercy of a fate over which they have no control. It is true that characteristics may be inherited from forbears and that these do influence the affairs of everyday life; but our fate is set, not by man, but by Divine Law. We are the sons and daughters of God and the inheritors of Eternal Life. However long the evolutionary processes may take, our destiny is to be pure and perfect as the Master Christ, Who became Man in order to teach us how to live. History reveals that there have been many who, in spite of lack of good parents, education, opportunity and health, won a place worth having in the world. They overcame a so-called "evil fate" by consciously, or unconsciously, applying Divine Law—they refused to be beaten. Through faith and effort they triumphed over inheritance and environment, and their lives have inspired many others to do the same. We are reminded by Spirit teachers that free-will in any world is not interfered with, and that before any Spirit enters upon another stage, it is aware of what that stage will exact. Those souls who are progressed often have the

hardest lives on earth, for the Spirit within them is willing to pay a heavy price for the great gift of experience.

FORGIVENESS.—This word used in connection with
the Creator is perhaps the one which misrepresents Him the
most. Over the generations people have been told that
God is Love, and yet in many prayers and litanies there
is a pathetic pleading for God to forgive man. How did
this contradiction arise? We have to consider the state
of mind brought about by ill-doing. Clairvoyant sight
reveals that, through the abuse of free-will, the wrong-
doer has closed his aura to the receiving of those Divine
rays which are always showered upon us; and until the
attitude of mind changes, the individual is shut off from
this Grace. Can this be rectified? Only by the one concerned realising that he has failed his better self when,
through regret, there arises a desire to atone. Because
man is God's child, instinctively the thought comes : "Oh
God, forgive me !" This change of heart unseals the aura
and the healing rays of the Holy Spirit can comfort and
uplift. We feel we must have forgiveness for wrong-
doing; God understands this instinct to be cleansed and
allows it, but He does not demand it. In the Lord's
Prayer the petition to be forgiven is linked to our forgiv-
ing wrongs committed against ourselves—another instance of the way in which the Father tries to help us, for
peace of mind must be absent so long as there is any
desire to "hit back." In spite of human limitations, when
we really love it is impossible not to forgive. How then
could God, Who is Love itself, withhold forgiveness until
we had pleaded for it?

FRIENDSHIP—the very foundation of happiness in
Spirit Life, where physical attraction does not exist.
True parental love is more closely associated with friendship than many realise, for both express unselfish service.
Some people regard this gift merely as something that
oils the wheels of life, and because its spiritual significance is not understood, the Law which governs its very
existence is ignored. We hear again and again : "My

best friend let me down !'' How do these tragedies happen? It is because the two concerned are not equally progressed souls, and often very elementary failings, such as jealousy or pride, can break those valuable links. Friends are brought together by Spirit agency for a definite purpose, and the earth-state is but a preparation for that wonderful co-operation which makes everything possible in the higher realms. Any form of "betrayal," because it cuts into trust, is difficult to rectify here or hereafter. Separation after physical death is due entirely to differences in spiritual unfoldment. Although we are able to visit those we love or they are able to visit us, we are divided from each other because we are keyed to different vibrations. Spirit teachers urge us to do our utmost to develop those qualities expressed by friendship, for without them we can do very little in Spirit Life.

GENIUS—implies an extraordinary ability to express with great power a talent or talents. The world owes much to these "sensitives," and had Divine Truth been understood by them, their gifts could have hastened the evolution of the earth far more than they have done. But mediumship in any form does not necessarily imply spirituality. Much that is good has been lost to posterity because genius (of the mind) has not been balanced by character (of the Spirit). We are surrounded by spirits in varying stages of progression. Highly evolved guides, who would gladly protect, cannot interfere with the free-will of the genius; and because such as these are so sensitive, they vibrate, often unconsciously, to every passing influence, seen and unseen, for the aura has not been stabilised by discipline. But if these sensitives sometimes fall to great depths, they are also capable of rising to greater heights than those who are less sensitive, as witnessed by the glorious music, etc., which has brought such peace and joy to humanity. "Temptation," in itself, is not a sign of weakness; the purest saints were subject to the fiercest temptations, but their love for Christ fortified their own strength and they mastered them. If a genius could be brought to believe that his handiwork would have far-reaching consequences on his life after physical death, the instinct of self-preservation alone would induce him to walk warily now.

GLORY.—Inspiration from wonderful sunsets and the great skill of artists have given us a faint idea of some of the emanations which stream from highly evolved souls in Spirit Life; but it must be remembered that the human mind is capable of vibrating to a very limited degree of that which we call glory, and this applies even to clairvoyants. Those who have clear vision know that the radiance and the multitude of colours in that radiance cannot be portrayed in language, for we have no adequate illustrations on earth. The aura of a holy one may extend so far that it covers a large room or even a hall. Sometimes the owner looks like a giant, for the aura keeps to the shape of the owner a foot or more from the actual form before it fans out. "Streets of shining gold" on the Other Side have been referred to, and some people have exclaimed, naturally: "I would rather have green fields!" But the "streets" are not made of gold; it is the atmosphere that may have given this impression to the physical mind of the seer. Nature in a greatly enhanced form, colours in far greater variety and beauty than the earth can show are there, and over it all there is a light rosy-gold atmosphere which recharges the visitor with an amazing vitality, this being, no doubt, the aura of that condition. If awe, reverence and humility are not aroused by visions of holy ones, then the clairvoyant has not seen what has been claimed, for the loveliness of their auric rays must cleanse us, anyhow, for the time being.

GREEN FINGERS.—This term is used in regard to those who have a great power over plants and flowers and, strangely enough, it is a form of mediumship possessed by many who do not believe in any kind of mediumship! It seems to be a healing power given for this form of life. Just as spiritual healers are able to build up the strength of those in the body, so there are others who can be used as doctors and nurses to Mother-Nature.

They perform, apparently without any special care, "operations" which would be disastrous if undertaken by others who have not the same power. Whether those with green fingers have a closer affinity with the Little People than the majority, is not quite certain, but it can be taken for granted that the Little People are quick to seize on the gift possessed by certain humans to aid them in their work for Nature.

GUIDES.—Spirit guides were intended by God to be ministering angels, and we all have them; but "like attracts like," and sometimes those in the Unseen who are less progressed are preferred by those in the body because they feel more at home with them. Here again we see how free-will can become a dangerous enemy. Many ask : "How can I tell the kind of guide I have?" The answer is shown by the life they live. Personal responsibility cannot be made the responsibility of any guide, for we do know the difference between right and wrong. There are some who turn to a guide whose form of encouragement is simply praise and flattery. If any guide tell us we are "wonderful" it shows that he has a very poor understanding of what is wonderful. So much support can be drawn from the Unseen that it is obvious that, in the main, we put up a poor fight over the troubles and trials of daily life. The progress of many guides is retarded because they are put first in the thoughts of those they wish to help. Guides are servants of God, as we should be, and according to their evolution, they are able to draw power from the higher realms. Individual guides represent but one in a long chain of spirits linking us up to the Godhead. We are meant to express our love and gratitude to them by doing the best we can, but directly we consciously or unconsciously put them before God, so are we injuring them. Guide-worship or saint-worship means a definite loss to the spirit concerned, and, therefore, is a poor reward for all they have done for us. All highly evolved guides entreat their instruments to go to God direct, through prayer, this attitude of mind allowing the guides to draw greater power in order to help those under their charge. As we progress, sometimes a guide will give place to another with more experience. There are many spirits of all grades around each one, whether it is believed or not; and the record of each day shows the kind of guides who have been influencing us, and this expresses, again, how we have used the gift of free-will.

HARMONY—is the precious link between man and everything that matters, for inspiration and other forms of mediumship are dependent upon it for good results. It is the key that opens the door to happiness in all worlds, and as man becomes more closely in tune with harmony, so are his higher faculties released. Harmony, then, is the power that represents the creative force which can turn the mundane into the ideal and, ultimately, the imperfect into the perfect. The harmony within highly evolved souls manifests itself in marvellous ways in Spirit spheres. They are so in tune with other forms of life that their presence not only has a stimulating effect on Nature, but actually provides the power to further its creation. We know a little about the wonderful "choirs" on the Other Side, and it is a fact that as a holy one passes through a condition, all the life included in a garden or a forest gives forth its individual note of melody—a manifestation, in sound, of the harmony between a son of God and the humbler creations over which he has been given dominion.

HEAVEN—a term used to express the abiding-place of perfect love and all its good gifts. Bound by the limitations of the physical mind, it is impossible for us to imagine such a state; but even while in the body our definition of happiness changes as we progress. In the Bible, Heaven or the Heavens are familiar terms used to express the brightness of the Spirit World, for many mediums of those times saw "the heavens open" or someone "ascending into heaven." The "higher heavens" were mentioned also, indicating that the seers realised there were different states of Heaven; and St. Paul speaks of the varying lights of the moon, stars and sun, "for one

star differeth from another in glory." Even the Summerland (a condition which can be entered immediately after
the transition) might appear to us as Heaven in comparison with the dimness of the earth. The assumption
that a separate state—Heaven—is the abode of God, has
arisen from the fact that Heaven is associated with perfection; but we know that God is everywhere and in
everything that has life; and all that is beautiful and useful in man and in Nature reflects, in a fragmentary way,
the glories and powers of those wonderful conditions, or
heavens, made possible by the love and service of God's
children, through His Grace.

HELL.—The idea of hell representing an unquenchable fire may have arisen in the human mind because in
olden days houses and bridges were built of wood, and
firemen, if there were any, had very little equipment for
dealing with it, and water was very scarce. So we have
a reason why an unquenchable fire became the greatest
punishment that could be inflicted. To-day man, in a
measure, is master of fire. But while we reject the thought
of hell-fire, we must face the fact that there are conditions in other worlds which represent terrifying hells.
These are not God's creation but are materialisations of
the cruelty and hate in mankind. By our thoughts and
actions on earth we build up our own "place" in the next
world; and it requires no effort of imagination to picture
the horrifying conditions brought into being by monsters
of iniquity who deliberately thought out means of tor-
turing the helpless people in their power. Fire, though
so destructive, cleanses a condition of disease, whereas
the materialisation of the awful emotions of these evil
ones literally brings into being diseases in a far fouler
form than anything the earth could show. We are reminded, too, that in the hells of man's own making there
are no helpless victims to experiment upon; all there are
equally cruel and bestial, and the warfare which goes on
among them, each trying to inflict the greatest injury on
the other, is beyond human language to express. But, in
time, through the inevitable suffering which such con-

ditions impose, a little spiritual strength is won, and missionary work can be begun. There are many varying stages in the different hells, according to the life lived by those whose "place" it is, and there they remain until a desire is roused for better things.

HOMES.—Family life in its real sense is a law of the Spirit Spheres, but the "family" represents those bands of workers who have been drawn together by mutual ideals. This does not exclude earthly love-ties, but it must be remembered that many brave spirits willingly undergo the discipline of living in inharmonious conditions during the earth stage in order to further their progression. Very often the antagonism among members of a family is simply a clashing of the auras; the one who seems to cause discord might have quite the opposite effect on others with different characters. But in the higher realms "families" are built up through the law of attraction, and so heaven, in degree, becomes a reality. In certain stages after physical death, houses represent homes, because those on earth have become so accustomed to the climate making protection essential that they cannot visualise a home that is not a building. But, as they evolve, spirits gradually lose their desire for things familiar on earth and so become prepared for higher states of revelation. A beautiful home in the Spirit World represents the highest form of happiness to the majority, and that home is assured until it is no longer wanted. But the family-spirit continues to grow ! Work on the Other Side is far more difficult than on earth, which is easily understood bearing in mind the adverse conditions which so many take over with them and the reconstruction which must be done. Only by bands of workers uniting in love and effort can sufficient power be forthcoming.

HONESTY.—The old saying that "honesty is the best policy" is a reminder that retribution is a fact although its action may in some cases be delayed. Honesty is associated chiefly with business dealing, but its spiritual aspect covers a far wider scope. There is honesty of purpose, honesty between friends, relatives and fellow-workers; and once it becomes a part of the individual's make-up they have the honour of being numbered among the sincere. Without the quality of sincerity we are un-employable after physical death, for there is no escape from truth in the After-Life. Flattery, dissembling, evasions, are all exposed in those conditions of Reality, and the dishonesties of the past are very hard to rectify because, in degree, they caused suffering to the victim as well as loss of trust in human nature.

HUMILITY.—Humility has a dignity which cannot be imitated; it is, as it were, the "hall-mark" of spiritual quality. It rests on the firm foundation of understanding which, again, came into being only by discipline. The gracious humility of the Holy Master, Who had all-wisdom and all-power, illumines life for everyone in whatever world they may be. Teachers from the higher realms remind us of the injunction to "test the spirits whether they be of God." We know that there have been spirits returning who have boasted of their power and influence. In the degree that humility is absent, so they condemn themselves and show their ignorance. The test of the spirituality of those in the body or free from the body is their humility and their willingness to work and to sacrifice.

IDOLATRY.—Idols may be associated with the past, but this temptation is always with us; it is simply that the character of the idols change. To-day they are repre-sented by intellect, material power, or possessions, and this form of idolatry is more dangerous than worshipping figures of wood or stone. Spirit teachers remind us that any prayer that comes from a trusting heart is accepted by God; the evils associated with idol-worship were the result of hypocrisy. The "heathen" were given a religion and they obeyed those in authority over them. In certain religions in this time, form and ceremony and even a beautiful cathedral can induce idolism. Among Spiritu-alists there is the danger of allowing guides to usurp the place of God or Christ. The commandment: "Thou shalt have none other gods but Me," was given for man's protection, as other gods have no power to protect his soul. Our Heavenly Father is "jealous" of them because He knows that idolatrous influences will undermine the progress of His children, and the consequences may be "visited upon the third and the fourth generation."

IMAGINATION.—It is not possible to "imagine" anything that one has not seen, heard, or had described while in the body or in the sleep-state; but our creative faculty allows us to re-assemble those things within our knowledge in such a manner that the result comes under the heading of "original." Imagination on a high level is as the hand-maiden of Spirit-consciousness, the mind of the greater self being freed sufficiently from materialism to pass on to the physical organ "inspiration." But imagination on a low level, through man contacting by free-will with astral or evil conditions, is responsible for morbid books, pictures and plays.

INDIVIDUALITY.—Personality is associated with the physical make-up; individuality with the soul of man. The development of character is by slow processes, and this applies also to the release of individuality. In the far past we were created by God in the Divine Image, but had to acquire personal experience. So the long journey through innumerable spheres in different "bodies" is essential, and as we learn the lessons of those many worlds through which we pass in our evolutionary stages, so individuality gradually is developed. During the earth state this is shown in little part by right leadership in all walks of life; but not until we become perfect as Christ is perfect can the full individuality of the God within us be expressed. (See EVOLUTION.)

JEALOUSY.—This failing was never meant to be the great enemy to peace it now represents. It examples the fact that evil is simply an inversion, or distortion, of good; and we are reminded by Spirit teachers that in due course it must be restored to its original holy state. To be jealous of another's good name or reputation is a protective instinct; and it can be a sacred emotion in a mother who jealously guards her children from contact with bad influences. But because human nature is evolved only to a limited degree in this world, jealousy has become a great menace to the growth of good-will amongst men. The difficulty in dealing with it in a constructive way arises from the fact that the emotion is so strong that it overwhelms reason; indeed, jealousy acts as a drug to the reasoning faculties. But when the mood passes the culprits are amazed that they could have been so blind to the truth. Those who understand psychic law know that, for the time, the one concerned is dominated by an earth-bound spirit who, apparently, is able to hypnotise his victim until it is too late to rectify on this plane the harm which has been done.

JESUS AND THE CHRIST.—"Do these names express one and the same Personality or are they two individual Spirits?" This is a question often asked. Some people believe that the bestowal of the Christ Spirit came only with the baptism of Jesus by John the Baptist; others that Jesus, the man, was but the medium used by the Spirit of Christ; others, again, that Jesus (known also as "Master" and "Christ") was merely a prophet with a magnetic personality and that His followers, being an emotional people, accredited Him with supernatural powers; and there are those who think that Jesus, out of vanity or lack of mental balance, masqueraded as the Son of God and, therefore, was a deliberate deceiver. But over the years there have been a great many earnest-minded people who have accepted as true the facts related in the Bible—that, according to the prophecies, in time a Child should be born of a virgin, who would be the promised Messiah—a manifestation of the Father given to the earth world in the form of Man, so that we should know that the Creator of all things in Heaven and in earth is a God of Love. And this is the teaching of highly evolved spirits who, by the Grace of God, are allowed to come back into this material state and to use those in a physical body as their instruments for the passing on of the Truth.

The baptism of Jesus signified that His missionary work had not only begun, but that the blessing of the Father rested upon it. This was after years of discipline in the home where, after the transition of Joseph, He was the breadwinner for Mary and her other children.

There are no facts to support the theory that Jesus was but a medium used by the Spirit of The Christ; indeed, in the Scriptures it is clearly shown that the conditions under which He was born were according to the prophecies in the sacred records. He was THE WORD MADE FLESH! His life, character and wisdom are far above any other example of love, humility and service that the world has ever known; and this is proved by the lasting nature of His influence, as well as by His power at the time to transform ordinary men and women into saints and martyrs. Over the generations there have been remarkable instances of Spirit Power manifesting through the gifts of mediumship; but when people quote Christ's promise that we shall do more than He did, so often they forgot the essential proviso—that in order to do so we must attain that high spiritual standard reached by the Master. This explains why no medium has ever been able to demonstrate the same holy power as that manifested by the Christ in so many different ways during His short ministry on earth.

Then another point has to be considered. In reply to a question as to what God was like, Christ said that "he that hath seen Me hath seen the Father (ST. JOHN ch. 14, ver. 9); also that "I and My Father are One" (ST. JOHN ch. 10, ver. 30); and before He entered the Garden of Gethsemane He spoke of the glory which He had with God "before the world was" (ST. JOHN ch. 17, ver. 5); and affirmed that God had given Him power over all flesh, even the power of eternal life (ST. JOHN ch. 17, ver. 2). These are extreme statements, and if they are not true and Jesus was not the promised Messiah, then instead of being a good man, He was a liar and a blasphemer. One cannot have it both ways ! Is Christ "the Way, the Truth and the Life"? Or is He, as some even to-day believe, merely a boaster and a fraud who, by mass hypnotism, became a dangerous disturber of the peace, and, therefore, had earned severe punishment?

When the Personality of Jesus was under discussion by the disciples, the Master asked Peter what he thought, and the reply came immediately : "Thou art the Christ, the Son of the Living God !" Jesus confirmed his inspiration by saying : "Blessed art thou, for flesh and blood hath not revealed it unto thee, but My Father which is in Heaven" (ST. MATTHEW ch. 16, ver 13-17). This is the true explanation ! The things concerning God and His purpose come by revelation only. A mind governed by "flesh and blood" cannot appreciate the full measure of the gift of the Light-Bringer, the Interpreter of God, Who by living under ordinary human conditions, became one with us in the experiences of physical life, and yet was able to show that although subject to earthly limitations it was possible to overcome all temptations. There have been other holy prophets whose influence has been enormous and they have been blessed accordingly; but Christ was the only One Who exampled PERFECTION during His life upon the earth plane. (*See* THE MESSIAH.)

LABOUR.—On the physical plane work seems to be divided into two sections—what a man does because he must, which often has a very tiring effect, and what he does because he wants to do it, for which a tremendous energy seems available. This fact illustrates the spiritual aspect of work. Much of the drudgery would be taken out of toil if, from youth, men and women were taught the truth : that even the most menial task done with a good-will has the immediate effect of creating beauty in the sordid conditions which surround the work, and this beauty does not pass away when the task has been forgotten. On earth, workers are graded into many sections, and untutored members of the professional classes feel there is a wide gulf between their gifts and the "common labourer." But in reality there is no difference at all; they are both meant to be workers in the vineyard of the Lord; the difference is made by man himself—whether he is a selfish or unselfish worker. So the Divine Law of equality is shown, and however much man's material mode of life may appear to upset the balance of justice on earth, the next stage will show that the scales have never wavered. Work, even uncongenial work, has saved millions from being engulfed in grief; in fact, it has stood between many of them and insanity. The capacity to work, there-fore, is a sacred gift; and if the spiritual consequences of any kind of labour could once be grasped by the toilers, the physical and mental strain which threatens to under-mine health, would be halved. We are reminded by Spirit teachers that the vibrational rate of life on earth is much slower than in the higher planes. Therefore, a busy life here is a valuable preparation for that greater activity which will be possible when the clogging influences of the flesh are no more. Men and women with very strenu-ous lives are ensuring for themselves great happiness in the World of Spirit, for they will not have to learn after the transition how to adapt their thinking powers and energies to the higher vibrational rate of an ethereal world.

LEADERSHIP.—Because leadership on earth is often associated with worldly ambition, its life is short, and it affords no preparation for leadership in the World of Spirit. There always will be leaders, but where are they leading? Spiritual careers of great promise have been wrecked by such trivial failings as vanity, the desire for power, and the refusal to accept the essential training for positions of responsibility. These instances are all too common in political, social and even in religious life, and such failures represent a great disappointment to Spirit guides and helpers, who have laboured over the years to prepare an earthly instrument for useful work. Again, it comes back to early training. If a boy or a girl is taught that it is right to wish to "get on," but that the develop-ment of character is the only way to safeguard ambition, then physical death would mean but an extension of leadership and all the joy it brings. Man is a son of God, and sooner or later he has to learn to LEAD in working, loving and sacrificing. In the planes of Spirit such leaders are wanted as badly as they are on earth.

LEVITATION.—The word implies that a being or an object, in defiance of the law of gravitation, is able to rise in the air without any seen assistance. Several instances of prophets and other holy people ascending in this way are chronicled in the Bible, and, relatively speaking, it was not an uncommon occurrence in other days of great faith and endurance. There are some to-day who can testify that levitation still takes place with sensitives when there is intense devotion in prayer. When a medium is controlled by a highly evolved Spirit it has been noticed by the observant that there is difficulty in the feet retaining a firm hold on the floor; the difficulty is overcome only by the will power of the guide. If levitation were allowed in public it would excite curiosity and draw in huge crowds who wanted to see the "exhibition." Spiritual guides avoid sensationalism; they seek to bring man back to God through appealing to his reasoning powers and dispersing his doubts by spiritual truth. The levitation of material objects, some very heavy, is well known and regarded as a demonstration of psychic force; but although proof can be supplied that such demonstrations do occur, no good object is served by them except, again, to rouse the curiosity of the onlooker. That same power, raised to a spiritual level, can be used for healing, and we have those who are desperately ill all around us needing this power. (See SPIRITUAL HEALING.)

MADNESS.—This terrible malady arises from several causes, but the wrong-living of past generations is largely responsible. There are those to-day who are in danger of insanity through heavy drinking and other excesses, and they are bequeathing misery to coming members of their family. Such as these have allowed themselves to become the dupes of unseen enemies who have gained an influence over them through the law that "like attracts like." In a very much smaller degree, grief is responsible for a deranged mind; also accidents. But in the main madness can be avoided by the training of character from early days, even if there is an inherited tendency to mental trouble. Self-control acts as an impenetrable armour to many evils, just as lack of it opens the individual to both moral and physical dangers. In the New Testament cases are cited of obsession by evil spirits, when the victim became dangerously insane. Knowledge of Spirit return and communion, instead of being the short cut to the asylum, provides the greatest safeguard that those in the body could possess. We are taught that thoughts are things; that deep depression and worrying, which are exhibitions of lack of trust in God, are to be avoided, for by ceasing to put up a fight against adversity we are handing the battle over to unseen enemies, and this may lead on to a subjugation which represents obsession. Life is difficult for the majority, but by filling the days with work, which prevents self-centredness, we are not only strengthening our powers of resistance against dark thoughts, but also we are bearing witness to the help received from the Bright Ones, who are there not to interfere with our experiences, but to bring us through such ordeals with an unbroken will. Mental balance, therefore, depends much more upon the character we have developed than it does on heredity. The asylums were full long before anyone heard of Spiritualism, many suffering from religious mania. It is the bounden duty of believers in this Truth, who know there are unseen enemies seeking to obtain mediums in the flesh, to be doubly on their guard; to keep a curb on their emotions and on unwise enthusiasms. We are meant to be "possessed" by the desire to serve Christ, not to be "obsessed" by entities who are working against the Divine Plan. Mental balance can be assured by keeping the many things of physical life in their rightful place, and that includes Spirit communion; it should not be allowed to absorb one's life, but should be sought only under prepared conditions. No highly evolved spirit wants to be tied to the apron-strings of the instrument he uses; he has other work to do, and so has the medium. We are working so that Christian Spiritualism shall represent a sane and practical religion, which can be put into practice by people in all walks of life.

MARRIAGE.—We are told by Spirit teachers that family life is part of Divine Law and this relates to all worlds. Long before the earth plane came into use for the purpose and the plan, God created life in "pairs." It is true, therefore, that "marriages are made in Heaven"; but free-will was given to man and will never be taken away. On earth only the few think of God in connection with marriage, and the majority never consider the effect it may have on their children. The law of creating—whatever it may be—is the law of love; and even if self plays a large part with earthly love, that degree of love does bring some protection to the soul. Pre-natal influence is a stubborn fact; and the observant find no difficulty in picking out those who are the result of a loveless marriage. The children may have great ability but the nervous system invariably is affected, and they find it very difficult to contact with happiness. They were born in sorrow—the sorrow of reluctance or regret that the right one was not there! Marriages of convenience are common; marriages for the sake of being married are seen on either side, also among the failures, and this applies to both sexes. The children, too, have to pay the price for the ignoring of Divine Law. And when there is physical attraction only, without mental companionship to bridge the gulf, the result is much the same. Rarely are the young given any practical instruction on what will make or mar their lives. As evolution continues the bondage of sex is loosened, finally to fall away, leaving God's children free to love without the heartache associated with it on earth. Gradually our love becomes refined as we progress through the Spirit spheres and ultimately, in the far future, we shall have so evolved that we are fit for re-union with that other "half" of our spiritual self, whose experiences may have been carried on in different

worlds from our own, but inevitably under the same Law
—service and sacrifice. That is "wedlock" in its true
sense. Spirit teachers emphasise that each one has to
learn how to become a true parent. If this is not part of
the physical experience, it is a reality during the sleep-
state, which is a very vital half of human existence.

MATERIALISATIONS.—Mediums who produce this
form of phenomenon are becoming somewhat rare, as is
the case with other forms of physical mediumship. The
power is now used more and more for spiritual healing.
The materialised forms of those who have passed over
are a fact, although it is a kind of mediumship that could
lend itself easily to fraud. The conditions required for
materialisations are not pleasant : although materialisations have been known in a dim red light, the usual
requirement is an inky-black room with no ventilation
(for fear that light should penetrate), which represents a
great strain to sensitive people. The medium sits in a
cabinet, namely, a "sentry-box" composed of wood or
heavy curtains. The forms of young people who manifest in this way are sometimes very attractive, but cruder
materialisation can be really repellent to sight and touch.
So much power is required to produce these forms that
there seems very little left for speaking. Just a few words
of greeting only are forthcoming in the majority of cases.
The forms are often some distance from the medium,
who is usually in a state of trance. They are seen by the
light provided by a luminous slate. Ectoplasm, like a
narrow stream of gauze, has been seen flowing from the
solar plexus of the medium, psychic force thus being
shown objectively. (See ETHEREAL.)

MEDIUMSHIP.—This subject is such a wide one that
the release of spiritual or psychic gifts represents but one
aspect, although a very important one. A medium is
simply a means of transmitting "thought" in various
forms to others in a physical body who, perhaps, are less
sensitive to that particular vibration : for instance, in
regard to music, or harmony in any other form, such as

singing or repeating beautiful words which, in themselves, are another expression of melody. Then there is
the great subject of invention. Marconi and others quite
frankly admit that their inventions, which have so bene-
fited the world, were simply a "brain-wave"—the idea
being impressed on the physical organ of the mind by
someone outside the physical range of life. They were
given the idea and then they, and others, had to develop
it and, by experiment, bring it into something of utility.
Parenthood also expresses a very fine form of mediumship, or the reverse; it depends upon the character of
those concerned. But what form of mediumship could
have more value than by example and effort to mould a
young mind so that the soul gains the protection it requires so badly during this material state? This applies
also to teachers and preachers of all kinds. Whether they
recognise the fact or not, they are mediums, and the
responsibility associated with mediumship will have to
be faced after the transition. The kind of mediumship
exhibited depends entirely upon the law of attraction, for
we are surrounded by a cloud of witnesses to freedom
or to bondage.

Mediumship associated with spiritual or psychic
gifts is also of a much wider character than is known
generally; a little study of the subject brings to light very
interesting facts. As the ages pass, the way in which
psychic gifts manifest may change, and this is a most
hopeful sign. In past years many kinds of physical power
were employed by spirits who had passed over, the object
being to force upon those in the body that there was
something operating which could not be explained by
material things. This kind of mediumship expressed itself
in a number of unpleasant forms besides ghostly apparitions. Damage to property was done or personal things
were removed from one room, or place, to another.
Sometimes a terrible "smash-up" was heard, but on dash-
ing into the room nothing appeared to have been moved
and certainly was not broken. Many have heard foot-
steps in a room, or up and down the stairs. Those who
do not understand these things do not know how to put

a stop to these uncanny experiences. Probably someone who had passed out of the body was trying every means of making his presence known, and if clairaudience were the gift of those in the body they would probably hear a message of good cheer—their love was just the same for those on earth, or they were trying to guide and protect them over the difficulties of physical life. These visitations are dying down now, and this is because more and more people believe in Spirit return and communion and, therefore, these friends of ours who are so anxious to get recognition know that if they exercise a little patience they will be able to pass on a message through a medium and so bridge the gulf between the two worlds.

The subject of trance mediumship is a very interesting one. We have those marvellous manifestations of Spirit power shown in the early disciples who were able to become "emptied vessels," as it has been described. This is the highest form of all mediumship. The controls were able so to use the physical casket of their instruments that they could walk among the people and talk to them, without rousing the dismay which the uninitiated so often show over trance mediumship, when the physical body seems either "dead" or in a deep coma. Spirit teachers are now concentrating on bringing back this form of mediumship, but it is a very difficult thing to do, for the complete co-operation of the instrument is essential, so that the body, vacated voluntarily by the owner for the time being, is left entirely free for use by the Spirit control. But the psychic gifts of the disciples alone could not have changed spiritual history as it was changed by their ministry; it was the combination of those gifts with the determination to give up all, if need be, rather than deny their Master.

Then we come to "inspiration," and it is impossible to say exactly where "inspiration" ends and trance takes place. Many of us have watched speakers, both in the pulpit and on the platform, who have had intermittent "control" during the whole time they have been speaking. It is as though the influence of the guide becomes so powerful that it is able to transcend the domination of the physical mind, and there is a flow of good oratory, which dies down abruptly when the speaker becomes self-conscious and feels he must fall back on his notes. And this takes place not only in public but in private life, people extricating themselves from the lesser mind in defence of a friend or of a principle. This means that the watchful guide has been able to get the "upper hand" of the normal consciousness because the one concerned has been animated by something of a higher order; and so a few blossoms are strewn on the dusty road of physical life. (*See* CLAIRAUDIENCE AND CLAIRVOYANCE.)

THE MESSIAH.—The title of "Christian" indicates that those who adopt it believe that Jesus of Nazareth was the Messiah Whose coming was foretold by holy prophets generations beforehand. A past President of the G.W.C.S. League, in his article on "Why CHRISTIAN Spiritualism" (THE GREATER WORLD October 6th, 1945), outlines the way in which we regard the Holy Master, and the following is quoted from that article :

> The Christian Spiritualist regards Christ as the only means by which we can know what God is like. Christ represents that accessible, understandable aspect of the Father that can be loved and whose example as Man, although representing an ideal, can be striven after God is in everything and over everything, and this fact brings a sense of separation between us—who are fragments of life—and God, the Source of creation ! The character and life of the Christ as shown during His earthly sojourn, may show up our limitations, but His loving kindness bridges the enormous gap between us and Perfection. We are not like Him, but we long to be; and we have His assurance that, through this desire, eventually we shall indeed be as the "children" of God, bearing likeness to our Heavenly Father.
>
> Very largely this awareness of the Divinity of Christ comes from an inner knowledge, a spiritual perception that cannot be defined or described, in the same way as many other spiritual experiences which cannot be "weighed or measured"—they just exist !

MIRACLES—events transcending the powers of the ordinary natural agencies but occurring in the physical world and capable of being seen by the bodily senses of human witnesses. The miracles narrated in the Bible are accepted by all who understand something of Divine Law, and rejected by others whose spiritual perceptions have not been released; yet the latter accept the miracle of creation as a matter of course. Miracles do happen to-day, as many can testify, and the only reason why they are limited in scope and number is because those on earth, by their attitude of mind and way of living, erect barriers between themselves and the operation of Divine Power. The horrors of war were outweighed by the tremendous effort and sacrifice forthcoming from those concerned; therefore miracles were made possible, such as Dunkirk which, if all the facts were known, might be found to be even a greater miracle than the parting of the Red Sea which allowed the children of Israel to escape. Not until the war was over were we told the full story of the miracle of Divine Grace which saved these Islands from annexation. That, again, was made possible only by the courage, faith and intense effort given out by the majority. Miracles are always possible through the co-operation of the God within man with the Spirit Power bestowed so freely by our Creator; but unless there is that co-operation they do not take place. Those who are working for humanity see many miracles, not of the spectacular type, but nevertheless so potent that the trend of a life is changed. The miracles wrought by spiritual healing do not concern the body only, but the mind and the soul; and the life of the one concerned bears witness to the fact. Where the tragedy comes in is that, through lack of spiritual understanding, many more miracles do not take place to turn this care-worn world into a realm of happiness and peace. "Within your own hands it lies," our Spirit instructors remind us !

MURDER.—This crime is a dreadful one, not only from the point of view of earthly law, but also because it is interfering with Divine Law. The earth plane is only one of many worlds in which the individual has the opportunity of acquiring experience, but it is of great importance because of consciousness of right and wrong. It must be remembered that we have had life in innumerable states before we entered the earth world, and because free-will was God's gift to man at creation, the spiritual self not only knows, but chooses its lot for each state, animated by the desire to hasten evolution. For another to cut short life on earth means a serious loss to the victim, quite apart from the horror of the struggle while the deed is taking place, and the trouble brought upon loved ones. Everything possible is done by the healers on the Other Side to readjust conditions after a violent death, but the next body is not completed, although when the aura has been spiritualised by an un-selfish life, Divine power can be gathered to it to form a substitute body.

But the position of the murderer, unless he was in-sane, is far more terrible, for not only has he to meet the earthly penalty of his act, but after the transition probably is earth-bound and suffers considerably because neither is his next body ready for him, nor does his aura offer the protection of the auras of more advanced souls. But this punishment, which the individual has inflicted upon himself, is seen as mercy in its highest form; for only by suffering can the lesson of self-control be learned and, eventually, the barrier to progression overcome.

MUSIC.—The use of instruments on earth and the effort required to master them, forms part of the training for the understanding of the Divine Law that governs melody. But the faculty of producing music here does not necessarily mean that the individual will be a music-maker in the spheres; it depends entirely on the influence exercised by the music produced. As the soul evolves, technical knowledge is superseded by aspiration. Those who during their earthly sojourn loved music but could not produce it, may be among those who can create the loveliest melodies in the next stage. The following inci-dent may comfort those who have had no opportunity of learning any musical instrument : A little girl, known to the writer, lay for two years in great agony from spinal trouble before her release came. Her one solace was a tiny musical box. She just had the strength to turn the handle and to listen to its three homely tunes. Now in Spirit Life that girl is able to bring into being exquisite music without the aid of any instrument. Some people, however, cannot imagine music without an instrument, and until they grow tired of its limitations an instrument is there for their use. Once they have seen what the love-rays of a Holy One can draw out of "Nature" and other forms of life, they realise that the source of music is within—it is part of the gift of our Divinity. The Law of Growth is harmony, and that is the foundation of melody. When there is real co-operation between workers it has been proved that success is assured.

NAMES.—Through the barriers created by our physical make-up, names or labels are an important part of material life and form the quickest way of indicating what we have in mind. And there is no doubt that this habit lingers in those states which are closely allied to the earth. But once Spirit-consciousness is released, then they fall into disuse except for the convenience of the less experienced. It is the same as with language. In other worlds there is a more direct method of recognising people and indicating things. In spirit spheres "we are known for what we are," which means that our individuality is so clearly expressed by our aura that names seem clumsy or misleading. Even on earth this is a fact in regard to places, houses and people. No doubt this is one of the reasons why mediums cannot always give the name most longed for. Mediums are not able to choose what Spirit condition they tune into : it depends upon their own vibrations; and only by exercising discrimination, which is developed by practice, can they produce the names desired. The other names given are not "inaccuracies"; there are so many spirits anxious to make themselves known that each one tries to get his or her name through to those on earth. Therefore, remembering the quickness of spirit sounds and vibrations, every sympathy should be offered to the intermediaries between this world and the next. Some names bring a sense of strength or, again, of fear or shame. This is simply an association of ideas, those in the past with these qualities or weaknesses having been known by these names.

MESSAGES FROM PEOPLE WHO HAD FAMOUS NAMES.—
Among the thousands of spirits who have spoken
through mediums in different parts of the world, sometimes a message is given by one who was renowned for
some conspicuous act or achievement in regard to his
fellow-men. Objection has been taken by some people
to the return of these famous ones, but, possibly, this
arises from a misunderstanding of Divine Law. In the
Spirit World the only greatness which is recognised is
that of "character." Many famous people became the
spoilt children of Fortune; but after the transition they
found that their position was entirely changed. The deed
which had been acclaimed as wonderful by those on earth
had lost its importance when seen among many acts of
folly or of selfishness. These once famous people often
tell us how much they had to work out; indeed the adula-
tion received from others over their "great deed" brought
temptations which they had found irresistible.

It is a great relief for these spirits to "return" and to
be able to warn others of the law of consequences, and
also to remind them of the transient life of earthly fame.

That pioneer Christian Spiritualist, Mr. Ernest
Meads, carried through an extensive missionary work
with those who were famous when in the body. In his
books he gave accounts of illuminating conversations
with many, including kings and queens of long past days;
and there is no doubt that his sympathetic understanding
brought them comfort and help. It would be grossly un-
fair if men and women who had well-known names when
upon the earth plane should be debarred from the privilege of returning and "talking things over" with those
who have spiritual knowledge; and their ready admis-
sions of failure to take advantage of their wide opportunities of doing good, rouses a compassion in their
listeners which acts as a healing balm to the suffering
caused by regret.

In regard to the return of the saints and martyrs,
again the question arises: why should the record of a
wonderful life of sacrifice debar them from making per-

C

sonal contact with those on earth who are trying to over-come their difficulties? In the Church of Rome petitions are made to these holy ones. It is taken for granted that these are heard by them; therefore they must be alive and able to act. And even if the petition is not granted as desired, the way has been opened for the one who asked in faith to receive God's Grace.

It will be found in Circles which have carried on their work over the years, that the earthly position of any spirit does not come into account. The spirits are allowed to use a medium because they are all children of the one Father; and very often men and women who were desperately poor, come through at the same Circle as those who when in the body had great power either through birth, fame or possessions. In the Spirit World it should be impossible for any kind of pride or snobbish-ness to remain because the record of past weaknesses and failures are shown in the aura.

NATURE.—This name covers a vast life upon the earth plane, but the beauties we see in sky, sea, hills and dales are but pale reflections of the loveliness of "Nature" in more evolved worlds. Nature on earth sometimes is presented in a distorted form, due to man's neglect or ignorance. Virgin forests, with their many dangers, show how dependent Nature is upon human handiwork. As stated in the Bible, God intended that man should have dominion over all other forms of life, but through losing dominion over his lesser self, that gift can be exer-cised only when there is a collective effort to harness the forces of Nature for the use of mankind. Nature in her loveliest form on this plane presents as much beauty as the human mind can assimilate. No artist could portray the beauty of even the outer courts of the Summerland, for on earth there are no kindred colours, "glory" form-ing the essence of the exquisite hues which are revealed to those with clear vision. It must be remembered that Nature as seen on earth represents but one phase of that vast life. The life within the seed of our great trees has already passed through many worlds, even as the Life within ourselves, and it will continue to express itself in ever-widening ranges of beauty and strength in those numberless states included in Immortality. It will be seen, therefore, how great is man's responsibility towards Nature, for he is both Nature's moulder and custodian; and in the degree that he does his duty to that portion of Nature which he contacts while in the flesh, so he will have won a fuller expression of this gift after the transition.

We read in REVELATION ch. 21, ver. 1 : "And I saw a new heaven and a new earth . . . and there was no more sea." In pictorial language this prophesied that the time would come when there would be no more division between heaven and the earth. The term "sea" was used because in olden days water was the great separator of man from man. Nation was cut off from nation because there was no craft which could ride the storms of the great seas. So the promise was given that the time would come when the gulf between earth and heaven would be bridged, and it has been fulfilled by the communion with the loved ones on the Other Side which is now taking place all over the world.

OBEDIENCE.—With many the thought of "obeying" seems to conflict with their ideas of independence. The roots of this reluctance go very deep in human nature, for over the generations those in authority very often abused their power. Between man and God the position is entirely reversed. God has given to man free-will, and this relates to pre-existence in other worlds as well as to the earth and life after physical death. In certain religions the Creator has been represented as a God Who demands obedience, and if this is not forthcoming famine and pestilence will be the punishment. But facts have proved that observance of Divine Law—doing what the Father has asked us to do—is best for us; indeed it is the only sure way to secure protection in its widest sense. But that is not a bribe : it is a "consequence." The greater the harmony between our lives and Divine Law the happier we are and, moreover, by this attitude of mind we are opening ourselves to receive inspiration from those in the higher realms. It is common knowledge that disease, war and destitution are with us to-day because of the abuse of free-will over the past, for man as a whole has misused his mind and body. Therefore the injunction to obey God does not mean that we are to be puppets; quite the reverse : we are meant to exercise free-will for our own evolution. It must be remembered that God never coerces His own creation. His Laws were instituted to help man to gain dominion over his baser self, when, as he evolves through co-operating with Divine Law instead of opposing it, he is able to release the powers housed in the Divinity within him for a greater expression of freedom and resource. Man, in persisting in having his own way incurs, through lack of experience, the consequences of his folly, and not only he himself, but others inherit the miseries that are associated with physical life.

OMNIPRESENCE.—We have the clear statement in the Bible that God is everywhere, and that He has the power of being present in every place at the same time. This fact may baffle the human mind if it is not remembered that God is in everything He has created. Divine justice is expressed in the fact that the Father's love for us is not forfeited by our wrong-doing; each one is loved in equal measure. Because we are sons and daughters of God we inherit a fragment of His unlimited power; and there have been many instances of men and women in the body manifesting in a clear objective form several miles from their own physical bodies. These are called "thought-forms," and they underline a great truth—that as man extricates himself from material entanglements he, too, in degree will have the gift of omnipresence, namely, will be able to manifest in more than one place at the same time. With highly evolved spirits this happens very often. Those with clear vision may see a loved Spirit teacher helping at one Service while perhaps he may be speaking through his own instrument at another gathering. Love knows no barriers of time or space, and where there are spiritual ties so it is the joy of these holy ones to give their help wherever it is needed. The writer has seen on several occasions such "solid" manifestations of a friend or relative that it seems it must be their physical presence and on checking up the time of these manifestations it has been proved always that the one seen clairvoyantly was thinking of the seer. Inexperienced mediums are warned of these occurrences so that they shall not jump to the conclusion that the one who so manifests has passed over. There is a distinct difference, and in most cases the clairvoyant sees that the "silvery cord" between the soul body and the physical body has not been severed. As we evolve, so the gift of omnipresence will become our own privilege, and after the fleshly body is discarded, by love and sympathy we shall in due course be able to help souls in different parts of the world at one and the same time.

ORDER.—Without the law of order, life could not be sustained in this or in any world. The amazing precision of Divine Law, even in regard to the material side of the Universe, staggers the human mind, and this is but an introduction to the precision which must be in action in regard to spiritual things. From the schoolroom to the great affairs of Empire, order makes all the difference to the harmony that prevails, and without something of harmony progress in any form becomes almost impossible. The cultivation of method and order in the home or in the office certainly "oils the wheels of life"; but even so, "first things must come first." There are those who never find any time for God's work because they have allowed material things to become their master; there are others who neglect both home and means of livelihood through deceiving themselves that Church work is the only thing that matters. Both are ignoring the law of order, which must include an observance of balance. Order, then, is as a companion to obedience; and when these qualities are absent the result is seen in disturbance and tumult, which may lead on to chaos. The brotherhood spirit demands a recognition of the value of order, and order provides the right condition for the building up of harmony, and harmony represents "heaven," for through its power all that is beautiful in life is brought to fruition.

ORIGINAL SIN.—Over the ages the majority of people have accepted the theory of "original sin," namely, that through the fall of the first man, Adam, sin was the inheritance of every child born into the physical world, in spite of the fact that it is impossible to associate transgression with a new-born babe. This belief led on to dreadful consequences, for if a young child died before being baptised (irrespective of the fact that there may have been no one available to perform the ceremony), the child's soul was regarded as "lost" or in hell. Moreover, the tiny body could not be buried in consecrated ground. This conviction is not confined to the "barbarous" ages; even to-day there are many who are terrified over the fate of a sick child should it expire before a priest or minister can baptise it. On the other hand, as far back as 400 years after Christ there was a monk, named Pelagius, who had the courage to refute the theory of original sin and, therefore, the necessity for the remission of sin by baptism. It seems incredible that good men and women could associate a God of Love with such senseless cruelty as to visit on a defenceless infant any kind of punishment, far less the terrible penalty of being lost for ever; yet such contradictions have been, and are, possible with certain types of mind. The doctrine of original sin seems to have been based on the idea of life beginning with the physical state, and that not until baptism takes place is there an "adoption" by God and the bequeathing of spiritual and eternal inheritance, but Spiritualists know that the earth life is one out of countless worlds which we live in before and after physical birth. Apart from this, even our limited capacity for compassion would reject the thought that the omission of baptism could make any difference to the future state of a helpless, suffering child. We know that the Father is Love Itself, and that when the physical body is too frail for this material world the little ones are gathered up by loving hands and taken into more ethereal conditions in the Bright Realms; and, as growth goes on, these Spirit children can, and do, return to this physical plane and, unseen by the majority, companion children in the body, learn with them and from them, and often are able to help them in turn. Another merciful provision is that during the sleep state loving parents can be with their children in the Spirit World.

(NOTE.—The story of Adam and Eve is a parable and not intended to be taken as a fact regarding the beginning of human life on earth. (*See* BAPTISM.))

PEACE.—Many peace-lovers find to their consternation that they are surrounded by disharmony, but life on earth would be all war if the peace-makers were not there. The true peace-lover is soon discovered. He has a calming influence wherever he goes for the peace within his soul makes retaliation or unforgiveness an impossibility where personal affronts are concerned; although he can be very firm when another has been victimised. A love of peace in no way represents a negative attitude. Of all things peace is the hardest to attain and therefore involves the greatest struggle, which can be forthcoming only from one with a positive nature who is prepared to pay the price for such a glorious gift. In the home or among friends there is the temptation to ignore wrong-doing "for the sake of keeping the peace." This may ease the situation at the moment but in reality it is adding to the armaments of war. We are meant to resist evil and to be ready to suffer for the faith that is within us, and peace is the reward that follows such battles for the right. Peace among individuals or nations is possible only by building up strength on the spiritual, mental and physical planes of life. Then God has instruments through which His Will can be expressed, and this Law relates to all worlds.

PERSECUTION.—The very word suggests an attack on something that is good, and although we pray for the persecuted our compassion is full of awe. Over the generations the world as a whole has been cleansed through the sufferings of the few who had ideals that were worth dying for, if need be; and their influence has been far-reaching. Our war-time hardships have lost their ugly appearance when placed side by side with the poverty and pain of those in the concentration camps; and surely some of these martyrs were able to build up endurance by recalling the lives of the saints of old and their courage to the very end. It is said that the strength of any religion rests upon the willingness of the upholders to suffer for its existence; and personal experience among our Churches has proved that sacrifice and suffering alone can produce that "power" which enables them to withstand attacks from material forces. Money and influence may have their day; but the test of any Church is its "staying power," and that staying power can be produced only by meeting the difficulties and obstacles with faith and overcoming them.

ARE THERE PESTS IN OTHER WORLDS?—In the parable relating to CREATION, it is stated that God gave man dominion over all other forms of life (GENESIS 1, 26)—the fish of the sea, the fowl of the air, cattle, and the creeping things of the earth. God is perfect; therefore every one of His thoughts which were materialised into form, must have been perfect also, and have had their part in the great scheme of Life. Nature on earth is in a fallen state; even so, the lesser creations do fulfil some definite purpose, although in some cases that purpose may seem crude or cruel to us. If this is so, it is the responsibility of man, for because he is the custodian of other forms of life, they are dependent upon him for their progression, and the disastrous effect of man's retrogression is seen on either side even in this world. But the earth state represents both loss and gain. Through effort and knowledge many things in Nature, dangerous to man, have been brought into subjection. This is seen in regard to swamps and fever-ridden forests. Civilisation may have its evil aspect because man

is still abusing free-will, but it has also brought much that
is good. It has opened out wide tracts of country for
people to live in and the diseases which once made life
impossible there have been brought under control, if not
entirely eliminated. The same Law applies to the owners
of fields and gardens. Man was intended to co-operate
with Mother Nature so that the soil should produce life
for the benefit of humans and creatures. In the degree
that a farm or garden is neglected so its usefulness
dwindles. Not only is the space occupied by weeds, but
the weeds choke that which is good, and so there is a
perversion of the power which was intended to bring
forth true life. Lack of cleanliness, whether through force
of circumstances or through idleness, is the cause of lice;
but how much worse must be the materialised results of a
really evil nature. Yet by personal effort and sacrifice
man can master all these enemy forces, for within him is
God !

This outline of truth applies to all worlds. Those
conditions which are less evolved than the earth contain
far more horrible witnesses to life in a fallen state; human
imagination cannot grasp the venomous creatures in the
hells of man's own making. Man has not only relin-
quished his dominion over other forms of life but, in those
awful conditions, is mastered by them.

In spheres which are more progressed than this
world no longer is there enmity between man and the
wild creatures. It is part of man's spiritual education to
penetrate into the "worlds" of other creations, to try to
understand the make-up of birds, animals, flowers and
trees. We are told that they all have their own language
and not only are these languages known by highly
evolved spirits, but also their separate personalities are
so well understood that they have regained "dominion"
over them, which is according to the Will of God.
"Dominion" over anything can be obtained only by love
and service, which means by helping these forms of life
to retrieve their usefulness, when no longer are they a
menace to man but a blessing. Therefore the good gar-

dener who by effort brings his plot under control, is in
training to redeem his power over the lesser creations.
The fact that his efforts do not produce what he hoped
they would, makes no difference at all. Nothing is lost.
The frustration of anything that is good on earth simply
means that these conditions were too crude to cradle that
which we would bring to life; but the "life" is blooming
in beauty and in power in a more ethereal state. Death
cannot touch man's spiritual desire; but sometimes the
only way in which the holy life within the seed can be
maintained, is to transplant it into a more suitable environment.

PHOTOGRAPHY.—At one time spirit photography
was much sought after by those desiring to obtain evidence of the nearness of loved ones who had passed into
the Beyond. Wonderful proof was provided in innumerable instances; and the fact that similar photographs can
be faked does not alter the fact that the majority of Spirit
photographs are genuine. Apparently it requires a lot
of practice from those on the Other Side as well as the
careful preparation of the medium; and various methods
are tried in order to superimpose the image on the plate.
Sometimes the most successful spirit photographs
occurred when least expected; and in other days they
came when the photographer was in complete ignorance
regarding their source. One disadvantage with these
photographs is that they do not express the present appearance of the spirit concerned, who long since has obtained a better "body." The images on the plate are
simply built up from the remembrance of what the individual was like when on earth, and that accounts for the
touch of crudity associated with them. Regarding our
loved ones in the Spirit World, it is helpful to them as
well as to us, if we try to visualise them with restored
health and beauty, and with a deeper intelligence and
understanding than could be possible when in the flesh.
It is this point that clairvoyants also should emphasise,
for "thoughts are things" and have a building power
beyond our imagination now.

PLANCHETTE.—This is a small board, usually heart-shaped, resting on two castors and the point of a pencil. The fingers are laid lightly on the board and with those who have that kind of mediumistic power, the board moves, writing letters and words. Many people want to take up Spirit communion in this way, but having received no instruction about safe-guarding the conditions, they become disappointed or even disgusted when what they regard as wrong messages come through. The great trouble with this form of mediumship is the "looseness" of the vibration which makes interference easy, not necessarily by an evil spirit but by one who is ignorant. Then there is the inexperience of the medium, who perhaps knows nothing at all about psychic law. For those who are determined to use the planchette the following hints may be helpful. Having prayed for God's guidance, do not ask questions; do not set your mind upon obtaining "evidence" regarding material things or people; keep quiet before you start and accustom those who sit with you to send out healing thoughts to the sick; then blank out personal desire from your mind and ask that what comes through will be for your spiritual guidance and upliftment. The writing may be halting, but the unseen visitor has to practise too. Do not sit for more than half an hour once a week; close with prayer and disperse quietly. You have to build up a "hedge" around you to protect you from interlopers, and this can be done only by observing Divine Law. If in spite of your precautions you find the messages are tending towards physical or material things, take your hand off the board and close with prayer. If next time the same thing happens, do likewise until, by your determination, you tire out the unwanted stranger. It is not wise to allow material messages to come through until a circle has been sitting regularly once a week for six months or a year, or even longer. All mediums whose mediumship has become absolutely reliable will confirm this. A careful note should be taken of the messages and the light of commonsense should be brought to bear upon what is said. It does not matter how simple it is, but if it expresses truth you are on the right path; if you get ambiguous language into which anything can be read, break the contact as advised above. In the early stages the guide who is allowed to use the earthly instrument is hampered by her inexperience. It must be remembered that free-will is never tampered with by a good spirit, only by one who is an enemy. Therefore if the medium wishes to know about material things, the guide has to stand back, and often a mischievous spirit gets a message through which causes a lot of trouble when proved to be incorrect. It is a case of "like attracting like." If the medium is determined to sit only for the highest and the best, the other end of the line of communication can be held firmly by the guide. But often it is not until the medium has learnt from bitter experience that it is wiser to abide by spiritual law that this affinity of purpose is established and, eventually, much good results. These warnings apply to all forms of mediumship. Much harm can be done by newcomers being told that they should sit to develop a certain gift if, at the same time, they are not told how to safeguard themselves from entanglement with adverse forces. When things go wrong with mediumship it is not hard to find where the weakness lies; and our first responsibility is that enthusiastic but inexperienced sitters should be told the blunt truth—that mediumship is perfectly safe when Divine Law is strictly observed, but it can be very dangerous if it is ignored.

POLTERGEISTS—a name given to psychic disturbances caused by earth-bound spirits. Generally it is found that in the household there is one who, though unaware of it, has mediumistic power of a material kind. Sometimes a lot of damage is done by breaking furniture or china, and great force is employed by such spirits to make known their presence. These entities are responsible for "haunted" houses and in the past have caused great fear among those who do not understand the continuity of life after physical death. In the effort to "lay" the ghost exorcising by priests has been tried, prayers being said and holy water scattered in the conditions. But the only really effective way of putting an end to these annoyances is to find a medium, experienced in rescue work, who will allow the restless spirit to speak through him. Once the spirit has come through, the reason for his troubled state can be traced and, by explaining his present position and showing how he can improve his condition, much good can be done. Often such spirits become useful workers. Because of all they have been through they are able to contact other bound souls and, with the help of those who have greater spiritual power, bring them out of the darkness into the light of understanding. Earlier in this series it was stressed that only very experienced mediums with strong characters are suitable to undertake "rescue" work.

POWER.—This word is charged with meaning to all Spiritualists; but it is associated with the things of the Spirit. Without the "power" mediumship could not be exercised nor could spiritual healing take place. From early stages the student is taught how to "build up" that power which is essential for everything in connection with Spirit Communion. When there is a breakdown in mediumship it shows that either the power is weak through lack of practice, or it is of a wrong kind. That is why we urge all those who are sitting for the development of their psychic gifts to be on their guard; to start from the very beginning to draw to themselves the right kind of vibrations which, in time, will enable highly evolved guides to use them. "Like attracts like"—this is shown with almost terrifying distinctness in mediumship. It is not that some instruments have holy guides through favouritism or chance; every soul has a holy guide seeking to influence them. But unless the condition is provided by the medium through the willingness to serve and to suffer, then more material spirits congregate around them until a better state of mind prevails, when the way is opened for the messenger of the Light. Spirit Power is the answer to what appears as a riddle to the uninitiated — why in some cases the revelation received through some Spirit Guides is of a much higher order than it is through others. But Spirit Power is manifested among those not classed as mediums—through the endurance of sufferers, through the faith of the heavy-laden, and through the courage of the poor! Terrible though the conditions of such as these appear to mortal eyes, clear vision reveals that around them is so much Spirit Power that loveliness in every form is in their surroundings.

PREDESTINATION.—Spirit teachers insist that predestination—instead of expressing fatalism, which has the effect of killing resistance to adverse circumstances—brings us the good news that in time we shall all be drawn into conditions of light and joy, and be so in tune with God's Will that we shall take up our inheritance as sons and daughters of the Most High. In the past perhaps too much stress was laid upon the wickedness within us and too little on the fact that man is a Spirit and, therefore, he is predestined to angelhood. Man was created in God's own Image, but he was without personal experience. The long journey through uncountable worlds in varying "bodies" represents states of loss and also of gain; for, through suffering over mistakes, at last understanding comes that the Laws of God are the Laws of protection for man, and that a wonderful future awaits him as he grows ready to receive it. Our fate is set by the fact that there is God within us, and the time will come when man's Divinity will be able to gain dominion over his lesser self. Then he will, by choice, collaborate with God and learn from his Divine Father how other forms of life are brought into being.

PRE-EXISTANCE.—(See REINCARNATION.)

PREMONITIONS, PRESENTIMENTS OR PREDICTIONS.—These words express the faculty to sense events or conditions that relate to the near or far future. People who know nothing about mediumship, as we regard it, have this gift and those around them recognise it. The word "fey" is used in Scotland in regard to those who foresee

death.   This ability to forestall time is a very interesting
one and leads on to subjects too deep to be discussed in
" nutshell " explanations.   Those who possess this faculty
can supply no reason for their feelings that a certain
thing is going to happen, but they can never be per-
suaded that they have made a mistake, which shows that
someone unseen has been able to impress the physical
mind very definitely with the image of that future hap-
pening. In many cases the gift acts as a great protection
or, if the event cannot be averted, as a preparation so
that when it does occur the shock is not so great. Among
our grandparents, who had never heard of messages
from the Spirit World, this faculty was shown sometimes
with great accuracy over future important events; and
it was regarded with respect by those around them. The
simple explanation is that spirit beings, according to their
state of progression are able to see what is going to happen as the years go by, and the mediums they use are so
in harmony with them that they can either borrow their
knowledge, or the guide impinges upon the physical mind
certain facts regarding what is coming to pass, and the
medium is able to pass on this information.

PROPHECY.—Prophets have a very rough time, for
the effect of prophecy rouses irritation because it is something that time only can prove to be false or true.   But
in the days of old either the teachers had greater courage
than we have or they were more responsive to the power
of the Spirit ; for the Bible is full of the most remarkable
prophecies which have been worked out. But at the time,
the statements made must have sounded so fantastic that
it is not surprising that authority stepped in and imposed
severe punishment to put an end to "such nonsense."   On
the other hand, there were always some who believed,
and if the prophecies were worked out in their own day,
then the prophet received full honour. But we marvel at
the faith of the spiritual teacher who prophesied that in
time to come "a virgin shall conceive and bear a son and
shall call his name Emmanuel—'God with us'." (The
prophecy is chronicled in ISAIAH ch. 7, ver. 14, and re-

ferred to in MATTHEW ch. 1, ver. 23, in connection with
Joseph's dream vision.) On hearing any prophecy, the
first question asked is : "What does it mean?" But if the
prophet knows, then it is not a prophecy, for it must concern something entirely beyond the range of the physical
mind. The prophet is defenceless if accused of deception
for he has no proof to offer as a justification; but how
poor this world would be if there had not been great souls
to brave the assaults of the earth so that "the Word of
God" could be passed on through them !

PRAYER.—Concentrated efforts are made by the holy
ones on the Other Side to impress the physical mind with
the consciousness that prayer acts as a sheet-anchor to
the blows of human life. What prevents the efficacy of
prayer is that too much, or even everything, is left to
God, and so little is forthcoming from the supplicant.
Reiterated prayer can become a meaningless jumble of
words, and clairvoyant sight reveals that very little is
accomplished by it in the way of opening the channel
between the individual and the Spirit Power which is trying in vain to pierce the density of the earthly aura.
Many of the "boys" have returned and given facts of
wonderful help received in times of intense danger and
difficulty; but they were exercising every grain of effort
and courage they possessed before, in their extremity,
the prayer was torn from them : "Oh God, help me !"
when the miracle was worked. This underlines the Law
that governs prayer, which is the greatest force in any
world. But Spirit teachers remind us that in the planes
of Light no prayer is unaccompanied by intense and sustained effort. That is the real meaning of the saying
"God helps those who help themselves." Those with
clear vision who have nursed serious cases of illness know
the difference made by the patient's attitude of mind. The
sufferers who are praying for patience and endurance
rarely realise the amazing beauty of the conditions
around them—the great waves of circulating power of
many hues; and the bright ones who, with unremitting
care, seek to draw off the fiercest pangs of pain. But that

is why eventually peace descends upon the physical body, and he or she passes into Eternal Life literally cradled in exquisite flowers, around which is an aura no human words can describe. The nature of a transition makes all the difference for good or for ill in regard to the beginning of a new life.

PSYCHIC PHENOMENA—things seen or heard by the physical organs which are super-normal, and because such phenomena are somewhat rare they arouse an enormous interest. This is a good sign because it shows that a vast number of people are not merely body; they have minds capable of appreciating the finer things of life. When a great Cross has been seen in the sky, naturally it is caused by cloud formation; but our sky is always full of clouds, yet only once in a long while are they used to remind us of the protection of the Cross. Thousands of people saw this phenomenon on one or two occasions during recent years and no scientific explanation could rob them of the comfort and reassurance it brought them. Phenomena operate on astral as well as on spiritual vibrations. The phenomenon of seeing a table spinning round the room is impressive; but a spiritual manifestation has the effect of a sweet and cleansing breeze, and a wonderful elation follows through that brief contact with holy things. Over the ages there have been many instances of psychic and spiritual phenomena; but the ones that never will be forgotten are those witnessed on the first Christmas Day, the Mount of Transfiguration, and the Ascension. But the important point is that the ordinary individual can be an instrument used for spiritual phenomena; and many people are able to travel in spirit beyond this plane of matter into ethereal realms and to bring back wonderful reports of life in other worlds. Those who once have witnessed a spiritual manifestation will never again be satisfied with mere psychic phenomena, which are like the dust of the earth in comparison with the Bread of Life offered to each and every one.

REALISATION—a faculty which allows us, eventually, to solve the problems of life. This gift is within the reach of one and all, and through it we are able to understand the necessity for discipline. Our realisation is limited only by lack of personal experience, for until we have actually been through sorrow and pain our minds are incapable of imagining what these tests represent. So it is seen how the troubles of daily life can become assets, because only through the realisation of what they exact from human endurance can the understanding come as to the way in which they can be overcome. Realisation, therefore, brings the power to gain dominion over adverse conditions; and this faculty gradually expands into Spirit-consciousness, when the Spirit within becomes so in harmony with Divine Law that adverse experiences are no longer able to erect barriers between us and God's Love.

"RECORDS" OF HUMAN LIFE IN THE SPIRIT WORLD.—
In regard to "records" the human mind naturally thinks of archives or vast libraries in which they are housed and wonders in which conditions in the spheres they would be found.   But in the Spirit World, language gradually loses the important place it has gained on earth, where it has become a necessity for reference, or for God's children to understand each other. We have been told that thoughts are THINGS, which means that they are manifested in colour and in form. A crude simile is the technicolor film by which stories of life are portrayed and can be reviewed at will. It is impossible to imagine that all our thoughts and actions are a permanency in any world; but it is reasonable to visualise man's Spirit-consciousness as a "scroll", that the events of our life are impressed upon it and, by Divine Law, are accessible at any time to act as an encouragement or as a warning.

The act of recording is automatic, in the sense that thoughts and actions immediately leave an impress upon our Spirit-consciousness, in the etheric conditions around us, and also they are shown in the aura. A cheering fact is that "good" has immortality, and cannot lose either its power or its strength; yet by regret and effort to do better, the impress made by those things which are "in-

verted" good or even bad can eventually be obliterated
and leave no stain upon the past. Like earthly habits
which are so hard to cure if the struggle is postponed, so
rectification of error becomes harder to achieve according to the gap between the committing of the fault and
repentance. For those who continue to struggle against
their weaknesses and apparently never are completely
successful in overcoming them, there is comfort. Spirit
teachers assure us that so long as we keep on trying we
are on the winning side and, later, we shall see that God
has completed for us what was beyond our own strength
to accomplish.

But with spiritually intelligent people the review of
the past is not held over until after the transition. During
the sleep-state progressive souls go back upon the events
of each day, and while the body is at rest, the higher self
is busily readjusting things by service in the Spirit World
or on the earth plane. The gift of omnipresence allows
the Spirit within us to go where it will in the degree that
the bondage of material life and the exercise of free-will
permit. It will be seen then that, after physical death, no
one need be faced with a terrifying accumulation of unwise or mischievous thoughts and actions—that might
well bring a sense of despair to the majority! The more
spiritual the individual the sooner the effort is made to
make good that which is hampering and damaging to
progress; and the sleep state can act as a levelling process; yet what is, or what is not, done during the sleep
state depends upon ourselves. Our life on earth, literally,
is building up our next body and also the next condition
in which we shall find ourselves; but those things which
appear so important to us while on earth may seem very
trivial when we are able to study at a closer range the Law
of cause and effect. Self-realisation is an experience of
first importance and must be faced in one world or another, and the capacity to "plug in" to the past is essential
to allow it to take place. While it may represent a terrifying ordeal to wrong-doers self-realisation to humble-
hearted people who have tried to follow the road of duty
brings an amazing revelation of the fulfilment of Divine

Law, which works on irrespective of physical and mental equipment, of environment or conditions. (*See* OMNI-PRESENCE.)

REDEMPTION.—A word which is charged with hope ! It implies that what has been lost can be found. It is not that man is expected out of sin and ignorance to develop angelhood, but a reminder that man was created in the Divine Image and, therefore, however much he may have desecrated his real self, within him IS angelhood; and it is only a question of shedding the gross matter in which Holiness is embedded for the beauty of the Spirit to be revealed. As explained under the heading of ABSOLU-TION, man is "redeemed" not by the blood-sacrifice on Calvary but by the love-sacrifice of the Man of Sorrows who, because He went through the temptations and trials of physical life, can enter into our struggles, and through His perfect understanding of the weaknesses of the flesh, can supply the strength that we must have to overcome them. In this way only can the precious gifts of peace and happiness, lost through the abuse of free-will, be "redeemed." Material force or authority has no power to win back those things which are of the Spirit; pure, unselfish Love, as offered by the Saviour of mankind, alone can work the miracle. But each child of God is asked to become, in degree, a "saviour" or a "redeemer" of others through the same power of Love. This is the Law that governs FAMILY in its spiritual sense, and that is why missionary work, which can be undertaken by one and all, is of first importance.

REINCARNATION.—A word used to express the belief that the soul has SUCCESSIVE bodies of flesh and, therefore, many lives upon the earth plane. INCARNATION means the entering of the soul into the body of flesh but once. Our spirit teachers affirm that we have but one fleshly body, although we have had innumerable bodies through which we have continued our experiences in many other worlds before physical birth. Bodies of increasing spirituality await us after physical death, as we progress through the Spheres, until ultimately we regain our likeness to the Divine Image in which we were created.

The Eastern theory of Reincarnation concerns the evolution of the soul and Karmic Law. The former is presumed to be effected by repeated incarnations in successive physical personalities, through which it lives and acts on the earth plane. Each time it resumes a body of flesh—after a rest, the duration of which depends on its evolutionary progress—the belief is held that it is drawn to surroundings which its own past has made necessary for its further advancement. In the Karmic Law of cause and effect it is claimed that the consequences of every act must be discharged in this or some future life on earth.

Let us for a few moments examine this doctrine in the light of the knowledge available to the Sages of old, who doubtless were as anxious to find out the Truth as we are to-day. They knew that the soul must return to God, and in the fervent search to discover how, they came upon the idea of progressive stages by which it would become gradually purified. There is truth in this part of the theory. But because they were ignorant of the greater World of Spirit and the innumerable spheres available for the soul's advancement, they conceived only the provisions of the earth plane and the return to earth as the one and only solution to their problem. It is almost certain that had these ancients the knowledge that spiritual understanding has brought us, they would have modified their views to harmonise with it.

Zodiac has stated repeatedly that we enter a physical body but once only. From him we learn, as from the Scriptures, that we were created in the Divine Image, and that in many other worlds and conditions we have travelled along the road of experience. Before we were progressed sufficiently to inhabit a physical body, we were able, as spirits, to walk with those on the earth plane. This truth is the key to the solution of many mysteries.

Mothers should have the definite assurance that the fleshly body of the child they have brought into physical life and on whom their love is showered, does not house one who has perpetrated evil deeds during a previous existence on earth. The SPIRIT of each child born into this world has knowledge of the tests and temptations which this stage of evolution must hold; but the physical life is started with the hope that the soul will be strong enough to overcome them. Wicked men and women represent a frustration of the Divine Plan for their lives on earth; but through the suffering brought upon themselves in the way of consequences, either in this life or in a future state, at last something of understanding is made their own.

The theory of Reincarnation raises serious barriers to Spirit Communion. Spiritualists believe that, by the Grace of God, if the right conditions can be provided, the void between this world and the Spirit Spheres can be bridged, and that disembodied souls do return to the earth plane and communicate with us. But according to the claims of Reincarnation, many of these souls may have started upon another life on earth, and, therefore, would be shut off from returning to the conditions of their loved ones in the flesh. Not only have the saints and martyrs spoken through mediums and given evidence of personality, but many souls who made serious mistakes during their earth life have also come back to tell us of the opportunities provided in the Spirit World for retrievement.

In studying reasons for rejecting Reincarnation it may be useful to consider the following points :

There are millions of "worlds." The earth represents but one short stage, important because of a knowledge of right and wrong which affords a wonderful opportunity for the Divine within to express itself.

The spiritual law which allows an individual to continue earth experiences after physical death, applies to the individual before physical birth. It is possible for an aspiring spirit to share the experiences of those on earth long before a physical body is available for it. This is why scenes and incidents outside the individual's experience during the earth life can be recalled at times by the mind of the body.

During the time the physical body is asleep, the spiritual self is free to travel in other lands and in other places. This, again, may account for the remembrance of places and people outside the consciousness of the material mind. In God's mighty Universe there are conditions in some of the astral worlds similar to those on earth and, therefore, the bodies worn there have their similarities to the body of the flesh. (CONTRIBUTED.) (*See* SLEEP-STATE.)

RELIGION.—This word originally meant the spiritual emotion aroused by belief in God. To-day a general question is : "What is your religion?" and we are expected to name a certain sect or denomination. Because of our mental limitations, on earth we find that labels are useful. But after the transition, unless we are still fettered by our prejudices, the realisation comes that real religion represents, not words—however beautiful they may be—but those deep and holy feelings which spur us on to sacrificial actions. In the astral planes (CONDITIONS BUILT UP BY HUMAN THOUGHTS AND DESIRES) people still separate themselves into different "religions," and for a time they are just as positive as they were when on earth that their interpretation of Truth is the only correct one. But religion in the World of Spirit expresses a wonderful freedom from mental bondage. We learn there by watching and seeing the working out of cause and effect; and we soon find that beliefs and pledges become a serious encumbrance unless the good thoughts outlined in them are put into action for the benefit of others. The Law of the Spirit World is LOVE; and the only way that Love can express itself is by service to others. (*See* ASTRAL.)

REPENTANCE —Often "a call to repentance" arouses resentment as it appears to be an interference on the part of God or His ministers with man's free-will. Repentance, too, is associated with humiliation—a public or private admission of wrong-doing which cuts deeply into pride. But, in reality, repentance opens the door to happiness and to the restoration of self-respect. The one who has responded to the temptation of envy, hatred or malice, soon finds that his dark thoughts are affecting his health and certainly have destroyed his peace of mind. The more serious sins bring worse results still. As injurious thoughts against others continue, so the injury to the thinker is harder to resist. God, working through Spirit agency, desires to draw the sting of poison out of the mind and to instill kinder feelings, when healing can take place. But free-will cannot be interfered with. The results of such thoughts lead on to acts of petty or serious revenge, or even crime. If the one concerned could be convinced that he is under the domination of a bound spirit, expediency alone would force him to make a tremendous struggle to throw off the condition. In these cases the gift of claivoyant sight offers a great protection, for once the terrible entity has been seen, no suffering or sacrifice would be too great in order to become free. People with clear vision do see these bound spirits hovering around the wayward ones, but self-will will not allow them to accept the evidence of the sight of another. Once pride can be overcome the cure is certain. God is Love! Our Heavenly Father does not want His children to go to Him in a grovelling spirit; but until there comes some consciousness of wrong within, it is impossible to draw the sufferer out of the tomb in which he has imprisoned himself. If only he would make even a little effort he would find Spirit helpers there to render first-aid and, by continuing his efforts, his spiritual health could be completely restored. (*See* VENGEANCE.)

RESURRECTION is the foundation of belief in a Living God. In Nature unlimited evidence is given of the law of resurrection; and yet over the ages hearts have been broken and lives ruined because that same law was not applied to man. A generally accepted belief was that the grave held the individual until the Judgment Day—whenever that might be—when the good went to Heaven and the bad to Hell. Enormous difficulties have arisen in the

human mind over the affirmation : "I believe in the resurrection of the body," which is echoed in that beautiful
anthem "The Messiah"—"and in my FLESH shall I see
God." But St. Paul made a definite statement regarding
different bodies—terrestrial and celestial—and had the
affirmation been : "I believe in resurrection in a body" it
would have been correct, for in the Bible there are so
many instances of angels or spirits being seen in a bodily
form, but the body was not of flesh. Spiritualists find no
difficulty in believing in immediate resurrection after
physical death; but the value of the teaching received
from Spirit guides is that they emphasise the importance
of the condition in which we find ourselves after our
resurrection. Have we a better body and a finer mind?
Or is our new body coarser than the flesh and our mind
less useful?

Regarding the physical body of Our Lord which was
not found in the tomb, many theories have been put for-
ward. The materialist may say that it was smuggled out
before the stone was rolled in, or that in the night the
stone was removed and the body stolen. But among
religious people there is also a divergence of views. Some
claim that through the great spirituality of the Master,
the fleshly body was disintegrated into the natural physical elements; others feel that as Jesus turned the water into
wine so a similar miracle was wrought upon the flesh.
But does it matter? What brought light into this dark-
ened world was the fact that after the Crucifixion He
was seen and heard and spoken to by a number of people,
and touched by one man at least; also that before His
ascension He gave forth further revelation regarding
God's plans for mankind, and promised definite help to
those who could find the courage to carry on His work.

RETRIBUTION.—This word to many suggests punishment alone, but in reality it is the gateway to freedom and
all it means. The law of "cause and effect" or "consequences" is logical, and is exercised for great gain as well
as for deep loss. The majority of people are not inclined
to learn from the experience of others; the gift of free-

will is there to be exercised as inclination directs. Yet
there are "results" which eventually show that goodness
attracts goodness and evil attracts evil. God cannot learn
our lessons for us; but once the truth is made our own,
no longer do we regard retribution as God's punishment,
but as a means provided by the Father so that, through
the suffering entailed by consequences, sufficient experience comes to avoid making the same mistake again. To
the looker-on it appears that retribution does not always
overtake the wrong-doer; but history shows that if retribution is delayed, when it comes it is of a very severe
character. Many people who try to live according to
Divine Law exclaim that if they diverge from it in the
smallest degree, punishment follows swiftly. That is a
sign not only of protection but of a progressed soul. Weak
thoughts or actions erect obstacles on the path of the one
concerned. These failures bring suffering, and in this
way they are worked out and do not hinder the pilgrim's
progress. Retribution, then, is among our greatest gifts;
it is really "readjustment" or "restitution," and a manifestation of Divine love and mercy.

REVELATION suggests the summit of spiritual
achievement; but during the physical stage our make-up
could not bear more than a limited degree of revelation.
And this privilege is within the reach of all, irrespective
of education, position or health; in fact, only the individual himself has the power to shut the door on revelation. And it has many aspects, ranging from symbolic
visions, visiting scenes of wonderful beauty, hearing
exquisite Spirit music, to the release of the perceptive
faculties which allows apparently ordinary people to
penetrate beneath the surface and to get to the heart of
things. "What shall I do to gain revelation?" many may
ask. There is one way only—the path of service and sacrifice! The greatest barrier between man and revelation
is conceit; until one falls out of love with self the Veil
cannot be lifted. That is why vain people disbelieve in
the revelation that comes to the humble-hearted. Helpful
and instructive as the gift of vision may be, we are re-

minded by the Holy Ones that in all worlds a greater gift is Spirit-consciousness which allows us instinctively to vibrate to Truth and, therefore, to be so in tune with God that we become co-operators in the Divine Plan.

THE SACRAMENT.—Shortly before the Crucifixion The Master invited His twelve disciples to meet Him in an upper room to celebrate the Feast of the Passover. He then indicated that their time together was growing short, and realising their loneliness after His physical presence had gone from them, He took the things of everyday life, bread and wine (wine being the usual beverage because of the impurity of the water) and instituted a simple Service in remembrance of Himself.

Over the generations this Service has been added to and adapted in order to meet the religious views of leaders of the various Churches To criticise the religion of another is inexcusable for it is the most intimate thing in the life of anyone. The attitude of Spirit teachers is this : that anything which helps the individual to feel in closer touch with God is blessed. This applies to rites and ceremonies and equally to Services carried out on the simplest lines. The one thing which does make all the difference is the love and devotion of those who partake in the Act of Remembrance. Through Holy Communion some people are able to overcome many barriers between themselves and God others find that eating the bread and drinking the wine, being a physical act, tends to break those delicate vibrations built up between themselves and Spirit life; others again confess that they gain no spiritual help from such a Service. It is a comfort to know that our Heavenly Father understands all His many children.

A point which has aroused much dissension is in regard to "transubstantiation," a belief held by members of the Roman Catholic Church and some in the Protestant Church, that the substance of the bread and wine is changed into the substance of the body and blood of Our Lord. To some people this theory is an essential part of their religion ; to others the claim appears as unnecessary and even repulsive. But the Holy Ones again remind us that things and ideas which appeared to be so important when we were in an earthly body, will be seen in a different guise when we are in Spirit conditions. Then all extraneous or outward things will sink into insignificance in comparison with what we really felt and did !

SACRIFICE.—This word when linked to religion often brings a sense of reluctance or shrinking; but acts of sacrifice are taken as a matter of course over the ordinary things of daily life. Many parents make tremendous sacrifices for their children, their homes and their gardens; but even over more material things habits are formed which express the essence of self-denial. The young who desire to take up a profession find that it is imperative that their mind should control their body, and overboard go amusement and recreation. Every serious student examples the determination to sacrifice the lesser in order to gain the greater. And it is this aspect of sacrifice which is associated with service to God, but here we have the certainty of exchanging restlessness for peace of mind, which is seldom the reward that accompanies gratified ambition. Those who have passed into the Greater Life come back with facts regarding the results of sacrifices made on earth. One and all make clear that what they "gave up" was but casting aside material substitutes for the real. Moreover, that by the instinct of sacrifice, or through having sacrifices thrust upon them, they became the possessor of many treasures of the Spirit. These, linked to the habit of effort acquired during the physical stage, mean that not only have they the opportunity of seeing the wonders of other worlds, but they have the power to do their part in creating them.

SEANCE.—*See* CIRCLE.

SEER.—A name given to one who foresees future events or who possesses second-sight. Second-sight is not necessarily the same as the clairvoyant vision. Sometimes the seer is conscious only of "feelings" or "impressions," and does not actually see pictorially the event prophesied by him. Many Celtic folk are "fey"; they sense or receive an impression that something unanticipated will happen—an accident or a passing. These foretellings are treated with respect by their own kind because past experience has brought proof of accuracy. "Fey" people, although they may know nothing about spirit-control, are really "sensitives" whose minds respond to the thoughts of those in the Unseen. Sometimes, if the warning is regarded, danger can even be averted through their gift. Then there are those seers mentioned in the Old Testament, prophets who generally told a wayward people what they did not want to hear! To-day many thousands of people believe in seership, and are willing to undergo a long training so that they may be used as mediums by progressed spirits to bring comfort and illumination to those in trouble upon the earth plane. (*See* PREMONITIONS.)

SENSITIVES.—All mediums must be sensitives, but all sensitives are not necessarily mediums in a Spiritualist sense. Sensitivity can be used in so many wonderful ways; in fact, inspiration is impossible without it. But individuals cannot be sensitive to certain things only—that is the trouble. They are responsive to all the conditions around them, both good and ill. Once again we are brought back to the exercise of free-will although we do not overlook the influence of inherited tendencies. But here it is that "character" not only shapes a man's destiny but also leaves its mark upon the world. How can the growing young be protected from the effects of their sensitiveness? Only by instilling in the youthful mind the law of "consequences" and by impressing upon him the obligation resting upon every talent-bearer. Artistic gifts of any kind to be of worth are founded on the sensitivity of the one concerned not only to receive inspiration, but to be able to express it! The responsibilities of those who are older and more experienced cannot be over-emphasised. How often we see and hear desecrations of Art and Music—manifestations of the kind of unseen influences around the composers or creators. If clairvoyant sight were possessed by such as these, they would be appalled to see the nature of their " inspirers." Little children, who normally are very sensitive, need far more safeguarding than they receive; and the damage wrought on their delicate auras by careless elders will exact much suffering in time to come from those who could have protected.

SEX.—Misunderstandings over sex throughout the generations have caused much misery, and we have been asked to give a plain statement of Spirit teaching regarding this matter, which has so great an influence on human life. But it is very difficult to condense the explanation into one short article.

Every child of God at creation, being an emanation of our Father and Mother God, must contain in their Divinity a fragment of the gifts and qualities which express the Godhead, which means that those characteristics associated in our minds with male and female must have been in their highest form in each individual soul; and we know that the perfection which ultimately will be attained by mankind represents the full DUAL development of the holiest qualities possessed by both sexes. The Master during His earth life exampled this in a wonderful way; He had all the firmness and endurance of a perfect man linked to the tenderness and understanding of a perfect woman. If this aim had been instilled into the young over the generations, what an amount of individual suffering, and even enmity between the sexes, might have been saved!

The distinction between male and female is shown throughout Nature, and their functions for the propagation of their own kind are according to Divine Law for this material state. People often exclaim over the repulsiveness of certain insects or creatures. They do not realise that the emanations from cruel and selfish men and women (in which the abuse of sex is included) are just as horrifying.

God's children are intended to be creative in a far wider sense than is possible upon the earth plane; but the METHOD of creation varies according to the stage of evolution reached by those concerned.

Thus we are brought to the Divine Law which governs creation, and that is LOVE. We cannot do anything well unless the best in ourselves participates in the process of bringing into being what we have in mind. This is shown in the Fine Arts, in all craftsmanship, and also in the ordinary tasks of daily life. Our physical restrictions make it impossible to say the degree of Spirit Power attracted by the various tasks; but we do know that the effort given forth, linked to the desire to benefit others as well as ourselves, will make all the difference.

So, from the creating of artistic and useful things, we come to the greatest gift of all—the privilege of providing an earthly body for a Spirit waiting to be born into this stage of experience to continue its evolutionary growth. The procreation of a child was intended by God to be the result of mutual love between the parents; but we know that there are those marriages which are merely pandering to the senses, or are entered into in order to gain money or position, and these provide the awful conditions under which many infants have been born.

Teachers from other spheres tell us that parenthood in the Spirit World is universal, and that this Divine Law is worked out irrespective of parenthood during the physical stage. In reality there are no childless men or women and no orphans, those in the Unseen, linked to us by mutual sympathy and love, being our children or our parents, according to progression. Earthly relationship which does not express the love-element ceases to exist after physical death. The great chain of Life, from the weakest to the strongest, is held together by the law of "family," the ones who are more experienced spiritually undertaking, as a parent, the care of those who are less evolved. Therefore to learn the lessons of wise parenthood while in the physical world can be a very great help in the way of preparing for parenthood in the great Life to come. (*See* FAMILY AND CHILDLESSNESS.)

SIN—expresses lack of spiritual development, a voluntary departure from what is right, and although retribution may fall upon the culprit, all sins have their repercussion upon others and, therefore, are in direct opposition to the brotherhood spirit. In thinking of sin, naturally we go back to the "fall" of man; and from the parable of Creation (given in GENESIS 1 and 2) we know that the "fall" came through disobeying God's command regarding the tree of the knowledge of good and evil, which stood in the centre of the Garden of Eden. This is how the parable runs: the serpent questions Eve: "God said ye shall not eat of every tree in the garden?" The woman corrected him, saying that they could eat of every tree but one, which they had been told would bring about their death (*the death of perfection*). The tempter reasoned with her, saying: "You surely shall not die, but shall become as GODS because you will know good and evil!" The temptation offered was to obtain the POWER associated with gods; and Adam fell through Eve passing on the same irresistible inducement. Over the generations it has been shown that the desire for power has been man's downfall. We have had it illustrated all too clearly by the two wars started by Germany, a great Empire whose citizens have unusual ability as well as the capacity to work. Their "death" as a great nation—the inevitable punishment which follows the abuse of power—but underlines the inescapable truth of the parable of the Garden of Eden. (*See* ORIGINAL SIN.)

SLEEP-STATE.—The dictionary describes sleep as characterised by complete or partial unconsciousness, but that concerns the body alone. Spirit teachers have shown us that the sleep-state can represent a time of great spiritual activity, for according to the measure of release made possible by a disciplined life, the Divine within us is free to go where it will. Probably the work accomplished by the real self while the body lies in sleep, is of far greater importance than that undertaken during physical consciousness On the other hand, it must be remembered that body and Spirit were meant to represent a co-partnership, the tasks of the earthly day bringing power to undertake more difficult work during the night; and these labours, again, producing strength for the duties of physical life. We all thank God for a good night's rest; but only a few have grasped the wonderful nature of the gift of sleep, when the higher consciousness can function unhampered by the limitations of the flesh. Moreover, it is the meeting-time for loved ones on both sides of the Veil. In this way not only are the links kept intact, but those undergoing their earthly experiences can watch the progress of their dear ones in Spirit life; and those free from the body can pass on strength and cheer to pilgrims from the earth plane. It will be seen, then, that those who have passed over many years ago will be as familiar to us as those with whom we live in this world. But the scope of the work accomplished during the sleep-state varies considerably, according to temperament and evolution. While the body is resting, those with missionary instincts undertake, with the help of others more experienced, responsible work among unprogressed souls. Many, too, are used by their guides as mediums for teaching those who are willing to listen. People accustomed to spirit-travelling during the sleep-state can bring back some remembrance of what has been done, the conditions penetrated, and the men and women contacted. Again, the real self, when released from the body during the hours of sleep may go, by the law of attraction, to other parts of the earth plane and minister to sufferers there. Some of these experiences have left such a deep impression that the physical mind has been able to pick up the vibrations of that place, and should the one concerned while in the body go to the part of the world visited during the sleep-state, the physical eyes would be able to recognise it. (*See* DREAMS, OMNIPRESENCE and REINCARNATION.)

SOMNAMBULISM OR SLEEP-WALKING.—We have been asked to deal with this interesting subject. A certain dread is associated with sleep-walking because in earlier days it seems to have been closely connected with hypnotism. Nothing could be more dangerous than hypnotic suggestion—the control of one mind over another— unless used under the most careful medical supervision. But fifty years ago mesmerism and hypnotism were popular subjects, and experiments were made between friends with the free consent of the subject who was to receive the thoughts or suggestions imposed upon his or her mind by another, or even by a group of people. It was also a popular turn at the music halls. But those who studied the subject realised how dangerous this practice could become; it was not only gaining control over the physical mind of the victim but was known to lead on to mental trouble and also to serious damage of the soul.

Sleep-walking can take place by hypnotic suggestion; but more often it is the result of the thwarting of a highly sensitive nature; the child or the grown-up obeys an instinct to do something it wanted to do, or to seek to remove a discomfort. For instance : children who are not warm enough in bed have been known in their sleep to come down the stairs, open the door of a room where several people are talking together, go to the fire, warm one foot after another, and then go back quietly to bed, still asleep. Always there seems to have been the instinct in others not to awaken, or in any way to disturb the sleep-walker, and there is no doubt that serious damage might result if this rule were ignored. During the sleep state the Spirit of the one concerned is not held by the flesh ; by the law of attraction it may be far away from the earth plane. Therefore to waken abruptly the sleeper would mean a terrible shock. For this reason it is most unwise to awaken any child except by the gentlest methods. Children asleep in a train have been roughly shaken when their destination has been reached, and the shock to the child is all too apparent. The parents can hardly be blamed because no one has told them of the danger such a drastic awakening represents.

An interesting point is that if sleep-walkers are not

disturbed rarely does an accident take place. They can
walk over difficult ground without stumbling and have
been known to tread on dangerous edges without a sign
of faltering, which would be quite impossible in a physi-
cally conscious state. This fact leads on to the question
whether sleep-walking has any relation to the trance
state. As the habit seems to be confined to highly-
strung, sensitive people, it is quite possible that "control"
has taken place, and this would explain the reason why
they can go almost anywhere without blundering or
hurting themselves, although their eyes are fast closed.
It is reasonable to think that these people, if properly
trained, would have made good mediums. Also—and
this is most important—if the psychic faculty had been
given the chance of expressing itself in its right form, the
nervous system of the child or grown-up would have
steadied down and, eventually, have become quite
normal.

SPIRITUAL HEALING.—Faith healing is as old as the
hills, and it is pathetic to remember how often in the past
the faith of the ignorant was used to bring them suffering
and misfortune. "Curses" have been responsible for
ruined health if not ruined lives; and witch doctors obtained control over their tribes simply because the people
had faith in their occult gifts. But this does not relate
only to primitive people; throughout the generations
there have been those who have exercised a hynotic
power over their followers, with disastrous results. All
this shows the great influence which our thoughts have
over our bodies and even over our careers. But we are
comforted by remembering that we are SPIRIT, merely
occupying a tabernacle of flesh for a short time in order
to undertake the valuable experience of the earth-world.

Spiritual Healing is a manifestation of faith on a
much higher plane, and this explains why the results can
be so wonderfully constructive. Men, women and children, "given up" by medical authorities, who know their
condition is beyond the scope of science to cure, come to
Healing Centres, very often brought there by fear of pain

or of approaching "death"; and again and again the
health of these sufferers has been restored, or so repaired
that life no longer is a burden to them. The number of
doctors who believe in Spiritual Healing is increasing;
and there have been those known to have said : "I can do
nothing more for you ! Why not try the healers?" This
spirit of co-operation should be fostered on both sides.
It is ungenerous for anyone to belittle the work of the
medical profession, which exacts so much in sacrifice and
effort; and there are definite signs among individual
doctors of a real appreciation of what is being done by
spiritual healers in many parts of the world.

The seeker may ask what happens during the "laying on of hands." It depends upon the make-up both of
the Spirit guide and of the medium used. As there are
diversities of spiritual gifts, so there are differences of
administrations, yet it is same Power which, in varying
degree, works through all. (I CORINTHIANS ch. 12, ver. 4-5.)

The Divinity within us was intended to act as a
channel by which contact could be kept with the Higher
Realms, and although that channel may have been partly
closed by our waywardness over the past and our limitations to-day, it remains a channel and, by practice, can be
used by those in the Unseen through which healing rays
can be passed to sufferers. The extension of the channel
rests with the medium; according to his or her humility
and devotion so in greater measure will it be possible for
the power to flow. Guides or mediums who state THEY
will cure diseases should be avoided; no guide or instrument can do this; they are merely intermediaries, part
of a long chain of helpers in Spirit Life, and God alone,
from Whom the power must come, holds the threads of
life and death.

From this there will be seen that there is a dividing
line between those who heal by the power of the Holy
Spirit and those who use the mental tools of mesmerism or
hypnotism, which in some cases appear to bring immediate cures. Spiritual Healing deals as much with the aura
as with the body; and it takes time to rebuild the delicate

fabric of the aura of the patient and to cleanse it so that it can receive, and pass on to the ailing body, the healing rays of the Holy Spirit. Jesus Christ, the greatest Healer of all time, did not attempt to heal everyone; but in the parable of the ten lepers He stressed the importance of those who were cured maintaining a spiritual outlook. (ST. LUKE ch. 17, ver. 12.)

"Absent" Healing demands from the medium still greater effort and dedication; but the cures of dreadful complaints brought about by the earnest prayers and concentration of healers and their helpers are irrefutable, as well as outstanding in number. This, again, shows that all divisions can be bridged by LOVE; that through the Divinity within us contact can be made with other members of God's great family wherever they may be; and, also, that when there is an active spirit of service miracles of Grace can be wrought.

The reason why there is so much suffering is because of the abuse of free-will in the past and in the present. Many with frail bodies have inherited certain physical weaknesses, and the conditions of their life may have accentuated them; but God's promise must be remembered in regard to the sins of the forefathers—"I will show mercy unto thousands of them that love me and keep My commandments!" (EXODUS ch. 20, ver. 6) And we know that every pang endured through the flesh will be transmuted into strength and grace for the body in the next world. Pain has its place in this stage of existence, for purification comes through suffering, and those who understand what can be inflicted by the physical body will be able to return to the earth as powerful healers. (See GUIDES, MEDIUMSHIP and PRAYER.)

SUICIDE.—Self-destruction would not take place if it were realised that separation from the physical body does not mean separation from the conditions which seem to be unbearable. For this reason the facts passed on from the Spirit World should be made known far and wide. We sympathise with those who are heavy-laden during the earthly life, but we should feel more sorry

for those who have destroyed a valuable tool—the physical body—because they find themselves still fettered to
the old conditions but in a more helpless position. Moreover they see then the Spirit help provided by their
Heavenly Father, and they know that if they had
struggled on a little longer the silver lining to their clouds
would have become visible.

"What is the punishment for suicide?" many ask.
Self-destruction brings self-inflicted punishment. God's
loving part is shown by the ministering angels who are
sent to help them. They do all they can to prevent the
act, but free-will cannot be interfered with nor the consequences which inevitably follow the abuse of free-will.
The aspiring Spirit within us enters into each different
world for the purpose of acquiring knowledge of the experiences associated with those states. It is not God's Will
that man should be tormented in any stage of life, but
that he should develop Spirit-consciousness in the same
way as the bud opens under the rays of the warm sun.
But life on earth is influenced very much by those who
lived here before us and those around us. The "sins" of
past generations and of our own are responsible largely
for intense individual unhappiness; but even so, through
the knowledge of the Spirit companions who willingly
share our burdens, courage rises again and again, and
history reveals that men and women have survived incredible hardships through their faith in God and a belief
that the heaviness of their cross would be justified in the
end. The justification is shown immediately after the
transition, for those who sow in sorrow reap in joy !

The tragedy of suicide is that it is not possible for
anyone to separate himself from the material life until the
span allotted for that experience is completed. Therefore
without the physical body, which makes the things of the
physical world tangible and possible, it takes longer to
acquire the experiences of this stage. Moreover it is very
hard to influence people in the flesh when they have no
idea that there are those unseen with them who are in
need of their active co-operation. But God's mercy is
shown by the fact that through the increased disadvan-

tage brought about by the loss of the physical vehicle, and the suffering so entailed, eventually rectification takes place, and gradually the soul-body—which was not ready as the one concerned passed over before his time— is completed through his own efforts and by the aid of others who have won Spirit Power. (*See* MADNESS.)

THE SUMMERLAND.—The condition expressed by this word conveys much to Spiritualists, but enquirers ask what it really means. "The Summerland" is an inter- mediate state for readjustment and training. We are told of the glorious flowers, the sweet-singing birds and the lovable creatures which are there.   It is the children's realm especially, but grown-ups are taken there, too, and in such conditions it is relatively easy to forget the sorrows and pains of physical life. But it represents a temporary resting-place only until strength is regained and the mind is attuned to the new life in Spirit Realms. Some regard it as their REWARD for a hard lot on earth and it is, but rewards are not permanent unless the same high standard of DOING is maintained.   That is where the difference comes in between the Spiritualists' definition of Paradise, and the view held by many that effort and striving end with the earth life. We know that all that is good must be intensified as we evolve; yet no longer do these trials represent adversity but opportunity. There- fore the strain and depression once associated with striv- ing and struggling is changed to joy and elation, for each difficulty overcome draws to us greater Divine Power. The Summerland is certainly not Heaven, and it repre- sents only the "outer courts" of Paradise, and Paradise leads on to the higher spheres and eventually to Heaven —PERFECTION ! Yet the Summerland holds as much love- liness and wonderment as we can bear until our con- sciousness is expanded by experience. The "many man- sions" referred to by Our Lord indicate something of the wide scope of Spirit Life; but any attempt to give num- bers to the Spheres is misleading, for this suggests hard and fast divisions similar to those in this world, and this is contrary to Divine Law. The only barrier which pre-

vents us entering higher conditions is erected solely by
our own limitations. We are keyed to certain vibrations
according to our spiritual development, and it would be
agonising to an unevolved soul to find himself in a high
spiritual altitude. But, on the other hand, the holy ones
can go into the conditions of undeveloped souls to
minister to them because they understand how to
"clothe" their own radiant aura so that no shock is felt
by their patients. (*See* HEAVEN.)

SUPERNATURAL.—This word, used so frequently in
connection with Spiritualism, expresses those things
which transcend or exceed Natural Law. But those who
have studied Divine Law realise that there should be no
line of demarcation between the natural and the supernatural, for within us is Divinity and in that spark of
Divinity, in miniature, are the attributes of God. Also,
that before we became part of a material world we were
citizens of a spiritual world and our ultimate Home will
be in the Celestial Realms. This universe is separated
from those realms only because its material conditions
cannot act as a receiver of more than fragments of purity
and holiness; but the fragments which do penetrate the
density of these conditions produce all the real gladness
which is on earth.

The point to emphasise is that man IS a supernatural being, and if at this stage he appears to be merely
a material being, it is not a lasting state. Also, that however gross may be the vibrations which surround us now,
because we are Divine, by a prayerful attitude of mind
and an effort of will, we can extricate ourselves sufficiently from material conditions to contact with those in
the higher spheres. If humanity as a whole realised its
supernaturalness, then the physical world would represent a little Paradise, and progression would be fast and
sure. It is through man's mental attitude of dividing the
material world from the Spirit World that barriers are
erected between him and the knowledge which leads on
to revelation. (*See* MIRACLES.)

SUPERSTITION.—This is not confined to unprogressed races, and the more the subject is analysed the clearer it becomes that many superstitions may have quite a practical foundation. The development of the mind does not mean the rejection of all that comes under the heading of superstition, but that some of these beliefs slip into their rightful place in life—to help humanity instead of hampering it by playing on the fear element in us. Primitive races seem to be very sensitive to the return of their departed ancestors and also to the presence of Nature-spirits. Because no explanation of psychic sights and sounds (which are taken as a matter of course by a developed medium) has been imparted to them, one can understand that their consciousness of these outside forces does bring a deep sense of apprehension, to which their emotions and imagination easily add real terror. In our own country, even in these courageous days, there are many possessing psychic powers who complain of feeling nervous even when kindly spirits come near them, and contact with those from astral conditions often means a dangerous shock to the nervous system. Many could have become good mediums had they been willing to submit to the training, but they were lost to the Movement through overwhelming nervousness. Therefore it is easily understood why a belief in demons and the power of witches has persisted among primitive races over the generations. The part of those who understand Spirit Return and Communion is to dissipate fear by giving a practical explanation of what is taking place, and showing that the intermingling of the so-called supernatural with the natural is logical as we are both flesh and Spirit.

Quite a number of superstitions are linked to the conditions of daily life, and the habits of birds and animals, and aspects of the moon, all have their place in the minds of country people; and what appear as merely superstitions to townfolk are really beliefs based on the experience of earlier generations and handed down.

Why is this, that, and the other supposed to be "unlucky," the enquirer asks, and generally the only answer forthcoming is : "Everybody knows it is unlucky!" But there is much more behind it than that. For instance, there is the old belief that it is unlucky to milk cows without washing the hands—just a simple health law to prevent infection being given to, or taken from the cows. That misfortune would follow the seeing of magpies probably was because these birds were destructive to crops. We have heard that it is unlucky, or lucky, to sow seeds at certain times, and the moon has its influence, too. Knowledge of probable weather conditions at these periods may account for this. The luck associated with seeing a black cat cross our path perhaps relates to those days when homesteads were few and far between, and the sight of a cat, which is a "home" animal, meant that human life was close by. The throwing of rice in this country is supposed to bring luck to the bridal couple; but in India rice is an important food, therefore such waste is regarded as certain to bring misfortune. The same principle underlies the spilling of salt or oil. These things were precious in olden times, and the fear-element had to be brought in to induce the careless to become careful. Sailors are superstitious over many things, but they state that this is the result of experience. Many would refuse to sail on a vessel if they knew there were no rats aboard. They claim that the instinct for self-preservation makes rats forsake a ship that will not reach land again, and no argument against this would convince the crew.

The lighting of twelve candles around a dead body was done to prevent evil spirits crossing the "circle of fire"; and this custom is a material illustration of a spiritual fact. A circle of earnest people whose thoughts and desires are upon holy things, creates a band of light or "fire," and entities of a lower order have not the power to penetrate it. "It is unlucky to speak ill of the dead." Many people say things in the absence of the one criticised that they would not say before them. There are no dead, and these remarks hurt and hamper their progression. Then there is the superstition that misers must return to the earth plane after physical death. We know this is

true, for their absorbing desire for material things has
made them earthbound.

Therefore it is easily perceived that over superstition
we have to divide the wheat from the chaff. Superstition
is wrong when its basis is a fear implanted by those who
desire authority over the masses and deliberately exploit
their ignorance. But there are those superstitions
which appear to be a cowardly attitude towards the
supernatural, and these fears can be swept away only by
the conviction that all Life is one, and that service to
others—progressed or unprogressed—is the Divine Law
that governs it.

SURVIVAL —Many people who accept the fact of
man's immortality do not believe in the CONTINUITY of
life after physical death; they favour the theory that
there is a great gap between the earth life and life in the
next world. But Spiritualists know that the transition
means only a change in state (and not a change in temperament or character), and that an active soul finds there
is no break in actual consciousness. Those who have been
through long illnesses or are severely depleted by trouble,
are often put to sleep for a while soon after the passing
in order to regain sufficient strength to function in the
Spirit World, but before this period of replenishment
takes place they all see a loved one or even the Master
Himself. And even when they are asleep—as with the
sleep-state while in the physical body—the Spirit within
is free to go where it will and often is hard at work. The
two important points to remember in regard to survival
are : first, that there is no suspension of activity when the
Spirit is released from the flesh unless those concerned
cling determinedly to the belief that physical death means
a long, long sleep, when they remain for a while in a state
of coma, as free-will cannot be interfered with. Even so,
in time the grip of earthly thinking loosens its hold, for
the Spirit within is not asleep. Secondly, the KIND of soul,
mind and body newcomers will possess. Only the one
concerned has had any influence over this, for we go to
our "own place," which has been built up by our life

upon the earth plane. The statement that "what a man soweth that shall he reap" often is taken as a threat; but it should bring joy and reassurance to those whose physical life has been so difficult. Irrefutable proof of survival is being received constantly from disembodied souls; also of the working out of consequences of past thoughts and deeds, for good or for ill, for happiness or for misery, in the next stage of being. (*See* SLEEP-STATE.)

STILL-BORN BABIES.—Many parents, after making most careful plans for the young life which is expected, have had to face what represents a terrible disappointment when the little one has "died" either before birth or at birth. But spiritual truth can do much to close the wounds in heart and mind. Spirit teachers tell us that many souls are waiting for physical bodies so that they may undertake the earthly experience; but through material conditions or inherited weaknesses of the body in one or both of the parents, birth into this world is not attained. But physical life is a fact immediately after conception takes place—it makes no difference how short a period the mother was able to carry the young life; the soul of the child had its link with the parents and also with this world. The physical body ONLY is missing from the home; the child in his soul-body is often there although he spends much of his life among the children of the earth, learning the lessons they have to learn and sharing their lot. Many mothers and fathers are amazed when the earth-life is ended to find on the Other Side their children who were still-born and those who were "lost" soon after conception. Evidence has been given through many mediums regarding children who were unable to attain physical birth, facts being supplied as to the time of their passing; and this has brought conviction of survival to many men and women ignorant of God's Laws concerning life after death. What joy fills the heart of each loving parent over the thought of possessing a child, or children, in the Spirit World, whose earthly bodies were too weak to be retained, or who, through some accident to the mother before or during the time when the birth was taking place, failed to attain physical birth ! (*See* CHILDLESSNESS.)

TEMPLES OF THE HOLY SPIRIT.—Our Lord used the word "temple" to describe the physical body when He prophesied that if the temple were destroyed He would build it in three days. While on the Cross, Jesus was taunted with making this claim; but on Easter Day the prophecy was fulfilled. St. Paul often used the same term. He asked his followers : "Know ye not that ye are the temple of God, and that the Spirit of God dwelleth in you?" And the question was followed by a grave warning : "If any man defile the temple of God, him shall God destroy; for the temple of God is holy, which temple ye are." (I CORINTHIANS ch. 3, ver. 16-17.) The word "body" is described in the dictionary as the "frame" or material substance as distinct from soul, spirit or vital principle. Teachers from the Higher Spheres tell us that we have had innumerable "bodies" or "frames," each one suitable and akin to the world or condition in which we have been continuing our experiences, and this law applies also to the present and to the future; that the flesh is but one kind of "frame" or "temple" which houses the Divine Spark of Life granted to us at creation. Man has the gift of Immortality; yet St. Paul says : "Flesh and blood cannot inherit the Kingdom of God." (I CORINTHIANS ch. 15, ver. 50.)

What is man's make-up? The generally accepted answer is "body, soul and Spirit." The fleshly body we can see and study; the etheric body, which is expressed by the aura, can be sensed by many but seen by the comparatively few; the Spirit, being of God, is invisible, but its influence transcends the imagination.

The aura is not something that only surrounds the physical body; it impinges upon the flesh, penetrates it, and is intended to act as a protective covering for the Divinity within us. The aura, in which is expressed the character of the one concerned, forms the basis of the soul-body—that next "frame" or "temple" which we shall inhabit in the world to come. In each following stage this process of spiritual evolution is repeated, the body we are using developing its own aura by the exercise of our attributes; and this in due course constitutes the next "body" or "frame" essential for a more spiritual world or condition; and so on.

Some people in a physical body have auras which have a magnetic influence, yet the owner may have a very material nature. The aura represents the "life-force" of the Divinity within us; yet because God does not interfere with the exercise of free-will, that "life-force" can be so desecrated that it can be used for ill, instead of for the greatest good, as intended by the Creator.

Christ said: THE KINGDOM OF GOD IS WITHIN YOU (ST. LUKE ch. 17, ver. 21). The human mind cannot grasp the significance of such a statement; but we know that because it is of God, the "spark" of Divinity within the temple of the body—terrestrial or celestial as it may be —must express Perfection and Completion. As children of God we inherit a fragment of all the unlimited gifts of the Godhead; but too much emphasis cannot be laid upon the fact that these gifts can be employed or misused according to individual free-will. (See AURAS and SPIRITUAL HEALING.)

THOUGHT-READING.—Various opinions have been given to explain thought-transference, but not until we pass into the Greater World will the law that governs this faculty be fully understood. But much depends upon the sympathetic vibrations between the one whose thought it is and the other who receives the thought. Experiments have been tried between friends living far apart with successful results; but in regard to two or more people unknown to each other being inspired with the same idea or invention, there is no doubt that this is Spirit influence. We are told that vast bands of experienced workers on the Other Side form themselves into concentration groups when it is essential to impress upon the physical minds of those on earth that a certain thing must, or must not, be done. But this method is not

reserved only for big things; to those in Spirit life nothing
is trivial that has good in it, and people in the physical
body who are interested in any particular subject, or
ideal, find that at the same time, or within a few hours,
they were all conscious of certain constructive thoughts,
which because many received them, eventually resulted in
a definite action for good upon the earth plane. Mind-
healing is practised by many who may not recognise the
gifts of the Spirit, but really it is a branch of Spiritual
Healing. If a strong and noble personality gains an influence over a mind weakened by illness, there can be
wonderful results; but mind-control by one out for power
and domination can lead to disaster for the victim. This
is why the character of doctors and all kinds of healers
should be above reproach, for severe consequences are
incurred by an unwise influence over the souls of others.
Many who do not understand Spirit control think that
evidential Spirit messages are the result of thought-reading; but it would be far more difficult to read the thoughts
of strangers at a meeting than to receive impressions and
facts from Spirit helpers: moreover, the difficulty of
recognising the entity described, because at the time the
thoughts of the one addressed are upon their own relatives, is a common occurrence; but eventually the spirit
is placed, although it may take hours or even days for
recollection to come. The influence of mind upon mind
is an absorbing subject for study and, rightly directed,
could be of the greatest assistance in hastening the progression of human life.

TRANCE.—(See CLAIRAUDIENCE, CLAIRVOYANCE and
MEDIUMSHIP.)

TRANSFIGURATION.—Those with clairvoyant sight,
which includes some who know nothing whatever about
Spiritualism, have seen others transfigured, sometimes
by a light so bright that the physical form has been lost to
view or into another personality, the Spirit guide, working through the instrument, being able to superimpose a
thought-form of himself over the physical body of the

medium. Remarkable instances of this kind have occurred, when imagination could have played no part in it, for the one concerned knew nothing of visions and certainly had never seen with his physical eyes the garments worn in the long ago by those of other nations. In the form of mediumship known as " transfiguration," another face appears so clearly over the face of the medium that sometimes those without clairvoyant vision can see it, and great is their joy when they recognise a loved one. Again this is a matter of superimposing the image of one on the Other Side over the features of the medium, whose face should be in repose; facial movements are not necessary. Some controlling guides, in order to disprove collusion with the medium, ask anyone in the congregation to sit on a chair facing the people, and these transfigurations are shown on their faces, in some cases a young girl appearing as a man with a beard or vice versa.

TRANSMIGRATION AND TRANSMUTATION.—Long before "Spiritualism" was thought of, the theory of the transmigration of souls was accepted by many mystics and philosophers as part of the great Plan of Life. As far back as 582 B.C., Pythagoras, who did so much to shape the thought of Greece not only in his own day but for a long time after, believed in the transmigration of souls into other worlds, and taught that at "death" each soul would reap what it has sown in its present life. But he went further than that, claiming that a man's form could be changed into that of a beast if his life had been bestial; and this brings in the theory of transmutation, namely, that there can be a change from one form, substance or nature, into another. In regard to transmigration or transplantation, it must be remembered that dying to one state to live in another world does not mean a change in character but only in the conditions in which the soul will carry on its experiences. In referring to "death," Paul said : "We shall not all sleep, but we shall all be changed" (I. CORINTHIANS ch. 15, ver. 51), a belief which is in harmony with his statement that there are bodies terrestrial and bodies celestial. The "bodies" or soul-coverings, must be attuned to the world in which we live, and the physical body is suitable only for this material world.

The word "transmutation" has been linked to aspects of Nature and creature life which at this stage are repulsive and dangerous; yet this but illustrates an INVERSION of that which, when created by God, was beautiful and useful. "The whole creation groaneth and travaileth together" (ROMANS ch. 8, ver. 22). When God made man He gave to him dominion over all other forms of life; but his "fall" through the desire for power and, subsequently, his abuse of free-will, necessarily had its repercussions on the forms of life around him. But as man gains mastery over his lesser self, so he will regain that "dominion," which was lost through his own fault; and in due course every form of life will, through his ministrations by thought and by deed, eventually show an evolutionary improvement; and as man struggles more and more to reach out for higher things, so in due course will the conditions around him and the forms of life in them, return to that state of perfection which, as a "thought" of God, they represented when created.

In parable-form transmutation appears in fables and fairy tales, where we read of humans who are sometimes turned into animals or birds. Many of these were written by those who were the mediums of their time. Mediums who to-day undertake "rescue" work know that in the dark spheres there are souls who have fallen into a lower state, even outwardly, than any creatures on earth. The terrible "bodies" of such as these are a materialisation of their thoughts and deeds in a previous existence, either in the earth-world or in one less evolved. But as transmutation can take place on the destructive side, the same law holds good in the way of Divine Grace. The "bodies" of God's children can become more and more etherealised, and the beauty and wonder of angelic beings, seen by those with clear vision, could not be described in earthly language. (See REVELATION ch. 16, ver. 13; also DEMONS, ELEMENTALS and FAIRIES.)

TREACHERY.—We are often asked as to the sin which will be the hardest to work out in future states. Sins against the spiritual side of our nature do not show the same obvious signs as material or fleshly sins, but that relates to this world only. Treachery, being an attack on the trust of another, may inflict far-reaching damage to the nervous system and to the soul of the victim; therefore it represents the gravest responsibility. At once we think of Judas, whose betrayal of the whereabouts of his best Friend, resulted in Calvary. But Judas' repentance was immediate, and there are many who hold the view that Judas' intention was not that Christ should be taken, but that His arrest would force Him to demonstrate those great powers which He possessed, and this would confound His enemies and establish His supremacy over them for all time. It is stated that after the Crucifixion and before the Resurrection, the Master ministered to Judas, who was in the hell of his own making. But throughout spiritual and national history treachery has played a large and dreadful part; in fact, destinies have been changed by it as well as the future of numerous individual lives, and the consequences must have been severe for the culprits. The essence of Religion is fraternity — the brotherhood-spirit — which can turn any world into a semblance of Paradise; but the only way to build up that beautiful condition is for man to keep faith with man, whether stranger or friend. Therefore it is of the greatest importance that the young should be taught to "keep their promises," as this forms the foundation of trust in its wider sense. If the habit is not acquired in childhood it is very seldom developed it in later life. This is why there is so much mistrust in the world to-day between nations, and also between workers, whose material success would be made far more secure by the observance of "a straight deal," whatever the matter in hand. For one individual to trust another and to have that trust betrayed either in business, friendship, or in closer ties, is to sin grievously against the Divinity within us, and the rectification is costly both in regard to "time" and in suffering.

THE TRINITY.—The theological definition is a three-fold personality existing in the One Divine Being—the union in One God of Father, Son and Holy Spirit. But it is impossible to limit God. God, the Creator of all things, necessarily must be in everything that He has made and also in all worlds. Difficulty arises in some minds over The Trinity because of associating certain forms of power or of action with three distinct personalities, but it is impossible to divide what is indivisible. Man is always faced with the impossibility of understanding the Infinite; our finite minds are strained to the uttermost to assimilate the knowledge even of the earth plane; and because of that limitation we need aids to gain understanding of God the Creator. The physical mind cannot comprehend more than a very few of the countless aspects of Light and Truth and Love which the Originator of everything represents. In order to bridge the gulf between the Whole (God) and the fragment of the Whole (our individual self) we must approach God through something we can understand. Therefore The Trinity viewed in this way is a great help to us. We stand in dire need of a loving Father's care; we long for help from Someone Who has been through the trials and temptations of physical life; and we must be able to draw upon some great Power in order to overcome our weaker selves. Here we have Father, Son and Holy Spirit—all ASPECTS of the Godhead. Through the gift of the Holy Spirit we find the power to ACT; it is as a Fire that not only burns up the dross in our human make-up, but through its link with the Divinity within, it supplies the power to turn ordinary men and women into heroes and heroines, into saints and martyrs. Man also has a triune nature : he is body, soul and Spirit. But is man limited to three aspects? This cannot be so, because if God the Father is unlimited, and within us is a Spark of His Divinity, in our small degree we, as children of the Most High, must be unlimited also. The physical mind could not grasp the innumerable aspects of God manifesting in the different worlds and heavens; and if there is to be a uniting of man to God it is essential to close the gap between the Creator and the created; and this can be done only by presenting to man those personal aspects of the Godhead which he can comprehend and love and seek to emulate.

THE UNIVERSE.—This word implies "all created things as a whole, not only our entire solar system, but all the other systems of which the fixed stars are but the centres." That is a comprehensive definition from the mental point of view. Spirit teachers have sought to extend our mental range through the agency of Spirit consciousness, and gradually they are unfolding that the Universe about which we can THINK is a very small affair in comparison with God's Universe as revealed to those who have progressed through the Higher Spheres. We are told that the millions of stars and planets which can be perceived through powerful telescopes indicate only a portion of the vastness of the entire Universe. Because we have no parallels on earth it is impossible for Spirit teachers to attempt to describe conditions except in those stages of progression which follow immediately after the earth-life; but we are told that in uncountable worlds there is LIFE in a fuller form than we can understand now, or in a lesser form than that shown upon this plane of matter; that the children of God and other creations have "bodies" or "frames" suited to the conditions there; and we are reminded that any state in which we find ourselves has been "built up" by us through the life we have lived in preceding stages. But this does not imply that disabilities or limitations during the earth stage arise from sins committed in a previous state of existence, or that physical and material well-being on this plane is a reward for well-doing in the life before. On the contrary; we are taught that the burden-bearers in this life are the spiritually strong souls, and that those who are less evolved choose an easier lot.

With this greater knowledge, the earth is seen in a truer proportion to the WHOLE; its importance is only RELATIVE to those who have seen, or heard of so many other spheres; therefore, the guides warn us not to attach too much importance to physical life, which is only ONE short stage of experience out of a multitude of experiences in other states of being. That God, Who originated all things, could "think out" one world only—the earth —is contrary to commonsense; and yet there are many people on earth who still believe that the earth is all that "life" has to offer to mankind, or that spiritual evolution cannot be attained except by coming back again and again into a physical body for further discipline. The earth-plane represents, in comparison with the Spirit spheres, but an elementary stage of existence; but because we are the children of God, His Universe is our "inheritance" and, ultimately, as purification takes place, we shall be able to enter, at will, states of joy and revelation inconceivable to the mind of the body. (See THE SUMMERLAND, SLEEP STATE and REINCARNATION.)

UNIVERSALITY.—It is hard to realise that in Spirit Realms religious sects or denominations will be absent, but what a relief this will be remembering the dissensions they cause on earth. Such differences are to be found in certain conditions in the next stage of life, but they are only a survival of earthly habits of thinking. The religion of the higher spheres is UNIVERSAL LOVE, which, by expressing itself in service one to the other, brings about mutual progress and happiness. This is a practical illustration of the Law of Equality in all its beauty and power. God's children are separated on earth by race, class distinctions, education and religion. But in the Spirit World leadership depends entirely on character, and character is developed only by undergoing and rising above those experiences from which we all shrink. The earthly career depends largely upon talents, environment, opportunity, and the stock from which we come. These restrictions have to give way to reality in the celestial spheres, where it is shown that we came from God, that our original environment was pure and strong; and that we all possess, in miniature, gifts like unto those of our Heavenly Father. This is Perfect Justice as ordained by Divine Love ! These facts promise everything for our future, yet free-will cannot be interfered with. But we can see how important it is in the present to concentrate on more unity between mankind—a true expression of the brotherhood spirit. Then the "competition" of this material state would be slowly transmuted into what it represents in the Spirit Spheres—those of all worlds competing to give out the greatest help to other members of God's great family.

VENGEANCE.—St. Paul, who had so many Churches under his care, wrote : AVENGE NOT YOURSELVES, FOR IT IS WRITTEN—"VENGEANCE IS MINE; I WILL REPAY, SAITH THE LORD" (ROMANS ch. 12, ver. 19). There are some who would question that if it is wrong for man to avenge, why does God promise vengeance? This relates to the law of cause and effect or sowing and reaping. Man has the right to exercise free-will, but he must be prepared for the results when he abuses this wonderful gift, for God cannot learn our lessons for us. Retribution is not punishment inflicted by the Father, but rather that man punishes himself, for by doing wrong no longer can he contact with love and peace. Through failing to understand the working out of Divine Law, those who have been injured by others are tempted to retaliate; but in failing their better selves they are incurring the inevitable consequences, and also are forfeiting consciousness of God's healing power which is at hand for every sufferer. Justice seems to be missing on earth simply because retribution does not overtake the wrong-doer in a way that can be seen by others, or there is great delay before it happens. But, naturally, the more progressed a soul may be, the swifter the retribution, because the aspiring Spirit within is anxious to overcome the barrier which the fault represents, and by the physical mind and body enduring swift punishment, the barrier is removed. But there are those in the body whose desire for vengeance for a real or imaginary wrong is so persistent that they strike back again and again, and yet there appears no outward sign of retribution. But God's Law can never be evaded, and their position is a very serious one. After the transition they will find themselves in those dark conditions built up by their thoughts and actions and there they must remain until the results of their actions are worked out—a very difficult task because the damage done may be far-reaching. It is to avoid such dreadful consequences that we were entreated to avoid personal vengeance. Retribution is sure—but it represents God's most merciful way of bringing about RESTITUTION. (*See* REPENTANCE.)

VIBRATIONS.—This word expresses so much to those who are "sensitives" because they are helped or hindered in a great measure by the "conditions" which are around them. One of the first things a medium has to learn is how to control, or rise above, unspiritual vibrations; in fact, to be able so to close-in the aura that almost a state of immunity is reached. But it takes a lot of practice, and many failures are experienced before this wise habit becomes part of the medium's armour. Hamilton Aide, the song-writer, wrote many years ago : "We are as harps that vibrate to a touch from stranger hands unconscious of the strings," which showed his own sensitiveness. Artists, musicians and writers are among those whose mediumistic gifts—though perhaps unrecognised by themselves—show that unthought-of "vibrations" play a large part in their lives. We are familiar in these days with the expression "sound-vibrations." This illustrates how harmony, or good reception on the radio, can be marred when there is interference from other wave vibrations. It is exactly the same with our mediums. Under sympathetic conditions a medium is able to contact with so much Spirit power that her trance and clear vision are remarkable; but on another occasion she may find it almost impossible "to work." Those who do not understand psychic law, hearing the medium for the first time may regard her gifts as very poor. This variability is noticeable in private sittings, too. One sitter may receive remarkable help and proof, but the next sitter with the same medium is so disappointed that her mediumship is doubted. Yet should another medium be tried whose vibrations are more akin to her own, there may be quite different results. The attitude of mind of a congregation or of a sitter has a tremendous influence on the exercise of psychic gifts. Vibrations of love and faith and the desire to help the demonstrator provides a wonderful power, and the reward is sure. How well the medium knows when she is receiving this most necessary co-operation ! Not only is she and her listeners happy, but also the Spirit guides of all concerned, who leave nothing undone to bring illumination and comfort to those on earth.

VICARIOUS SACRIFICE OR THE ATONEMENT.—This is a term used by those who believe that the sacrifice of Christ on Calvary can be regarded as a substitution for the penalties incurred by sinners. This is a direct contradiction of the reminder : "BE NOT DECEIVED ! GOD IS NOT MOCKED; FOR WHATSOEVER A MAN SOWETH THAT SHALL HE ALSO REAP." (GALATIANS ch. 6, ver. 7.) Also : "WORK OUT YOUR OWN SALVATION." (PHILIPPIANS ch. 2, ver 12.) From the commencement of the communications from Zodiac he emphasised that this must be so; that only by personal experience can we extricate ourselves from mental and physical bondage, for God cannot learn our lessons for us, and this rules out entirely any suggestion of a substitute to suffer for our sins. Calvary would have left no mark on history had it not been for the love and purity of the Master's character, for crucifixion was a common form of punishment in those days. Christ, possessing Divine Power, could have saved Himself from the Cross; yet had He done so we should have lost a Perfect Example of forgiveness and patience under suffering. That the "blood-sacrifice" should be considered by some people as having a greater influence on mankind than His "love-sacrifice" is incredible to those who have studied Divine Law. Things associated with the physical make-up have only a transient life; whereas love, faith and hope remain for evermore. Our personality changes during the long journey of experience, but our individuality—the Divinity within—is unchangeable and has life everlasting. God has given us free-will, and if we abuse the gift we must suffer the consequences; but as our bondage lessens, impetus is given to our struggles against weakness by the remembrance of the Master's life and how He, although having all-power, voluntarily allowed His enemies to have their way. God the Father kept His promise that free-will, however much abused by man, should not be interfered with, and so the crucifixion took place. But probably nothing more would have been heard of this act of base ingratitude had it not been that three days later Christ showed that physical death was conquerable. For forty days before His Ascension He manifested among those who loved Him, and He instructed them as to their future work and of the dangers and difficulties associated with their task (ACTS ch. 1, ver 3). (*See* ABSOLUTION and CALVARY.)

VIRGIN BIRTH.—Some people find it impossible to believe that Mary was still a virgin when Jesus was born, although this fact is plainly stated in the New Testament. It was the working out of prophecies given through God's holy prophets generations before. We quote one of the prophecies : BEHOLD A VIRGIN SHALL CONCEIVE AND BEAR A SON AND SHALL CALL HIS NAME IMMAUEL (meaning God with us) (ISAIAH ch. 7, ver. 14). In Luke and Matthew we read that an angel appeared to Mary and prophesied that through the power of the Holy Spirit she would be the mother of the Son of the Most High, Whose kingdom should have no end. Joseph, too, saw an angel, who explained to him that it was a miraculous conception so that One should be born Who would save the world from the sin which was engulfing it. The angel asked Joseph to go through the marriage ceremony with Mary, but directed that the marriage should not be consummated until after the Babe was born; and it is recorded that Joseph obeyed this instruction. Remembering the great miracles performed by Christ, and even by His disciples, it is difficult to understand why anyone should find it hard to accept the fact of the Virgin Birth, or that it should be considered beyond the power or the imagination of God, Who created not only the physical body, but everything in the whole

Universe. Those accustomed to Spirit teachings know that the physical method of producing human life is for this plane of matter only. Necessarily there must be a variety of ways of creating life in the different spheres. We have passed through many worlds before physical birth, and there are innumerable conditions before us. Because there is Divinity within us, as we evolve we shall be able to create, INDIVIDUALLY, life in many forms. In this stage we know only a fragment of what could be expressed by the creative faculties of mankind. The "Immaculate Conception" does not refer to the Virgin Birth, but implies that Mary was chosen to be the mother of the Christ Child because she herself was miraculously conceived and born without original sin. There is no suggestion of this claim in the Bible, and it was not until 1854 that it became part of the dogma of the Roman Catholic Church.

VISION.—The gift of vision operates in many ways and upon many planes of being. The fact that several mediums at the same Service all see different things, offers no evidence against the faculty; it merely shows that instead of vision being automatic, it reflects the individuality of the medium. The prophecy in Isaiah that the young should both prophesy and see visions, indicates the link between the two gifts, for future events are often portrayed by "living pictures," witnessed by clairvoyant sight. Records of these visions appear throughout the Bible, and have been proved to be accurate prophecies. The seers of other days met with much persecution, which sometimes ended in a violent death. To-day many people who have never had a vision believe in the visions of others. Their gift of vision is of the mind and the soul instead of physical or psychic sight, and the fact that mentally they can visualise the scenes and people described by clairvoyants, shows that something of Divine consciousness is released. There are others who deny that these visions are possible; to them they are "hallucinations," simply because they have never experienced anything of the kind themselves. Some people cannot think of anything outside the range of their own experience, but as their experiences increase, so will their imagination expand. The great trouble every seer has to contend with is that earthly words are totally inadequate to describe the radiance of the Spirit World and the variety and delicacy of the colours there. With Spirit vision it is as easy to see over, through, or under anything, as it is to see the side which faces us. The same enlargement of view applies to the water-courses, the lakes and the seas. Colour-rays beyond human imagination vibrate through the waters, charging them with power, and the ripples or the gentle waves offer no hindrance to those who walk over, or upon them. (*See* CLAIRVOYANCE, COLOUR, and SEER.)

WAR.—We know that discord in any world is against the Will of God, and that Our Lord urged us to forgive unto seventy times seven. And yet Christ did not hesitate to expose wrong and to speak in the plainest terms to the evil-doers of His own time, an act which brought a terrible war upon Himself. The explanation of these two aspects is given by Spirit teachers and must appeal to commonsense. We are asked by our Heavenly Father not to retaliate when a personal wrong has been done, for the Divine Law of retribution and compensation is always in action. "Vengeance is Mine; I will repay," saith the Lord. But in the Gospels we are not instructed to stand aside when the helpless and innocent are oppressed and ill-used. If we do this, certainly we are denying the family-spirit. All processes of growth involve struggle or a warring against conditions. The fierce battle for existence shown in Nature is an illustration. Fighting with mechanical weapons is but one aspect out of hundreds of aspects of war and many who condemn this kind of fighting do not hesitate in private life to wage the bitterest war with their minds and the baser side of their natures; yet the sin of hypocrisy was the one which Christ condemned more than any other. Did not the Master name the Pharisees serpents, hypocrites and whited sepulchres? (MATTHEW ch. 23, ver. 13-33.) The

Christian must participate in all battles against wrong, whatever personal loss may be involved, for this is the only way of assuring more spiritual conditions for coming generations. Martyrs there must be, for evil is rampant all over the world. Those involved in the conflict find their actions misconstrued by others who take the course of least resistance; but such warriors have their place in the Christ Army. They go to war to put down evil things, and they are prepared to sacrifice all on the physical plane in their love for their brethren. Had not our boys been so inspired, to-day we should be the slave-workers of the Nazis, and the horrors brought about by their temporary domination would have become permanent. (*See* VENGEANCE.)

WEDLOCK.—(*See* MARRIAGE.)

WINGED BEINGS.—Many question whether highly evolved Spirits really have wings, and the question is not easily answered because "pictures" so often are used by those on the Other Side to convey a certain thought or meaning to our crude physical minds. This method is according to Divine Law because in the Spirit World (which is around us as well as beyond our present conditions), thoughts, feelings and desires are actualities; in other words, they are transmuted out of their mental or emotional state into fact. On earth they seem to be merely the forerunner of something that may, or may not, be materialised. Mediums who possess a high order of spiritual vision have seen "angels" (or as much of their loveliness as earthly limitations allow) and they are certain that there are winged celestial beings. The fact that over the ages angels have been portrayed with wings surely is evidence that seers from olden times onwards, have had visions of them in this form; yet still we do not know whether the wings are really part of their celestial body, or are shown to convey to our minds that such advanced spirits have reached so high an altitude of spiritual progression that they can go where they will in the Heavens. But these visions do not imply that only those who have wings can overcome space. Distance and time do not exist in Spirit Spheres, and when a soul is sufficiently evolved to vibrate to holy conditions, all limitations are conquered.

When fully conscious in a physical sense, the writer saw a great number of angels providing a corridor through which came the Presence Form of the Master. They were charged with holy power, which radiated all round them. The wings appeared to be of the softest down, in perfect proportion to the body, reaching from the shoulders to the ankles. Several inches above their heads the Light of the Holy Spirit was shown as a cluster of small "jets." Their glistening white robes, of a far finer texture than any silk, also vibrated with power. (See ANGELS.)

WITCHCRAFT.—In other days the punishment for witchcraft or sorcery was death, generally by burning, and it is estimated that there were 30,000 victims. During the reigns of Henry VI to James I, 3,000 were executed on the charge of witchcraft, the last victims in England being a mother and a child of nine, who were executed in 1716. In the reign of George IV, witches were graded among rogues and vagabonds, and the lighter penalty of imprisonment was imposed. Witches were accredited with supernatural power; in fact, they were supposed, with the help of the evil forces, to be able not only to foretell forthcoming events, but also to afflict people and animals with terrible diseases. In those days no one knew about the simple laws which go far towards protecting health to-day, and lack of medical knowledge made it almost impossible to save life. Serious losses among cattle caused by disease also added to the superstitious terror of the people. In their ignorance they looked round for someone they could blame; and those whose make-up was in any way different from the majority easily became "witches" and, inevitably, met a terrible end. It was one word against a crowd of people whose minds, for the time being, had become unhinged by fear of the dreadful illnesses for which in those days there was no cure.

Some opponents of Spiritualism regard mediumship as witchcraft, and many have quoted the story of King Saul and the Woman of Endor (I SAMUEL ch. 28, ver. 7-25) as a Biblical forbidding of the use of supernatural powers. But the Rev. G. Vale Owen related the true facts of this incident. He wrote :

> The word "witch" is not in the original text. It was put into the heading of the chapter by the translators in 1611 to please James I, who had written a book against witches. In the text she appears to be a lady of means and refinement and a talented psychic. Saul does not come out very well. He goes to her under an assumed name and, in return, she treats him as a gentleman, giving him hospitality. Saul does not see the form of Samuel, who appears to the lady clairvoyantly. The description she gives, however, convinces Saul that it is Samuel and no other. Then she gives him Samuel's message, either by trance, being controlled by Samuel, or by clairaudience. The message is a stern one, as Saul deserves. Samuel does not mince matters, and events prove that what he said was true. Saul is killed in battle the next day ! There is no condemnation of the woman from beginning to end of the narrative.

WORK.—(See LABOUR.)

WORSHIP.—This word is now used so freely that it can express the greatest reverence, or just another form of human desire. The worship of idols was forbidden by God in olden times as those in authority used these graven images in order to deceive and to rob ignorant people. But ALL sincere prayers are accepted by God. To-day there are those who are equally idolators; they worship the mind, riches, beauty or power; and with some the concentration on the coveted object is so great that they have been willing to barter everything else to acquire it. But even in regard to the worship of God, there has been some confusion of thought over the ages as to what it really means. Religious leaders laid down that it must be expressed by hours of prayer and mental striving, accompanied by acute discomfort; and only when the will had lashed the emotions into a state of ecstasy had a state of real worship been achieved. But the reaction of even religious emotion is, generally, depression, the reason being that the feelings have found no expression in active doing.   Thought and emotion play an important part in Life as a whole; but they represent but the soil from which can emerge the blossoms of ACTION. Therefore worship is incomplete, however great the sacrifice entailed, if not extended beyond the range of "feeling"; in other words, Divine Law ordains that it is impossible to serve God unless we serve our brethren. So the value of worship is limited in the degree that the emotions do not lead on to useful action. (See IDOLATRY.)

ZODIAC.—In the dictionaries this word is associated with the twelve constellations. Our teacher has always described himself as "a humble servant of the Master," but because those in the body need a name for spirit visitors, he chose "Zodiac" because it would lift our thoughts from the earth to the Heavens. Identification in the Spirit Realms, we are told, depends upon the difference in aura. In response to an earnest entreaty many years ago, our teacher told us a little about his earth life. He revealed that he was the unnamed scribe whose conversation with Our Lord is chronicled in ST. MARK ch. 12, ver. 28-34. This scribe—who had noticed that the Master had answered well those who sought "to catch Him in His words"—asked which was the first commandment of all. The answer given by Jesus expresses the essence of Religion—THOU SHALT LOVE GOD WITH ALL THY BEING AND THY NEIGHBOUR AS THYSELF. The scribe (whom we now know as Zodiac) exclaimed that that which the Prophet said was true, and added that it was "more than all burnt offerings and sacrifices." Whereupon Jesus, perceiving that the scribe had understanding, replied: "Thou art not far from the Kingdom!" We read that after that "no man durst ask Him any question."

Zodiac was a teacher in the Temple at Jerusalem, and his open partisanship of the new Prophet who was attracting so much attention, was regarded as a serious crime by the Chief Priests and Elders; moreover, he had openly belittled the time-honoured custom of burnt offerings and sacrifices. The result was inevitable. No longer was he a venerated teacher at the Temple; his symbols of office were torn from him and he was turned into the streets as an outcast. Zodiac joined the disciples. He witnessed with them the Crucifixion, which followed shortly afterwards, and also was among those who saw the Risen Christ. After the Ascension, the little company—the first Christian missionaries—divided up, going to different parts of the country, travelling long distances on foot in order to spread Christ's Gospel of Love. Sometimes they were received kindly, but more often the spies sent out from the Temple at Jerusalem had reached the hamlets and villages before their arrival, and they were greeted with stoning or beating and driven away. Zodiac has said that death came near them so many times that when at last he was slain (probably by stoning), he did not know the physical end had come. Hedged in by enemies, worn out by hardship and poverty, these valiant "shephards" using crooks for climbing, trudged over the hills and down into the valleys trying to find the few who would listen to the Truth. If some seed fell by the wayside, much must have been sown on good ground, for in time there were thousands of men and women who were willing to sacrifice all for the faith that was within them.

The Inspired Teachings of Zodiac
from The Greater World Association Trust

THE ZODIAC MESSAGES (Reference Edition) compiled and arranged by A. H. Hillyard

In this volume of 395 pages of actual text some 69 of Zodiac's most outstanding addresses on important subjects have been annotated and indexed for easy reading and study. They concern the great Scheme of Creation; the Evolution of the Soul; the Purpose of the Earthlife; Free-Will; Predestination, etc.; and are in simple language and terms easy to grasp. We commend this beautiful and inspiring book as your treasured companion.

THE ZODIAC MESSAGES (Non-Reference) Vol. 1 compiled by F. N. Tolkin

This book contains 30 Zodiac Addresses on important subjects: Auras; Animals; Suffering; Reincarnation; Christ the Judged; The Holy Spirit; Telepathy, etc.

THE ZODIAC MESSAGES (Non-Reference) Vol. 2 compiled by F. N. Tolkin

Companion to Vol. 1, contains 32 Zodiac Messages on, The Greater World of Spirit; The Friends of God; The Era of Revelation; The Uses of Adversity, etc. The above two books are beautiful and instructive.

THE PRAYERS OF ZODIAC compiled by A. H. Hillyard

In response to public demand a collection of Prayers of this wise Teacher have been produced in one volume. A blessing in one's private devotions, and to those who speak the word of God in public.

Christian Spiritualist Classics from:
The Greater World Association Trust

THE TABERNACLE IN THE WILDERNESS or The Reality of God in the Physical World (Illustrated) by A. H. Hillyard

The Tabernacle was the Tent of the Presence of God in Israel. It constituted the great experiment of government of a people by Divine means alone, and was a type and foreshadowing of the time when the Kingdom of God shall be established on Earth.

THE MINISTRY OF ANGELS by Joy Snell

A beautiful book dedicated to the Bereaved. Mrs. Snell was a hospital nurse and she describes her visions in the wards of Spirit helpers ministering to the sick.

THE LIFE BEYOND THE VEIL by the Rev. G. Vale Owen

Vol. 1 – The Lowlands of Heaven
Vol. 2 – The Highlands of Heaven
Vol. 3 – The Ministry of Heaven
Vol. 4 – The Battalions of Heaven
Vol. 5 – The Outlands of Heaven

Given by progressive Spirit communication through the hand of the Rev. G. Vale Owen in the vestry of his Church at Orford, Lancs. These books are classics of great spiritual beauty. They describe in these fascinating narratives life and progression in the Spheres Beyond.

PAUL AND ALBERT by the Rev. G. Vale Owen

What happens to those who have lived selfish, cruel and depraved lives on earth? Here, through the hand of the Rev. G. Vale Owen, is an authentic account of conditions that apply in these nether regions.

EXCURSIONS TO THE SPIRIT WORLD by Frederick C. Sculthorpe

A remarkable book of visits to the Spirit World. His faculty of astral projection is unique and makes fascinating reading.

MORE ABOUT THE SPIRIT WORLD by Frederick C. Sculthorpe

A worthy follow up to Excursions to The Spirit World.

BOOK LIST

A comprehensive Book List is available from the Greater World Association Book Room, 3 Lansdowne Road, Holland Park, London W11 3AL, England.

PUBLICATIONS

The Greater World: A weekly Spiritualist journal based on the Christ Teachings.

The Childrens Greater World: A monthly magazine for children of all ages, useful for the home and Sunday School.

Specimen copies sent on request.

The Greater World Association Trust,
3 Lansdowne Road, Holland Park, London W11 3AL, England.